To Bob Thompson

Keep hunting alive!

Jeff Jordan

3/8/2019

Home to the Brave

Remembrances of war
brought home to
one small dot on a map

Jeff Jardine

Home to the Brave

Remembrances of war
brought home to one small dot on a map

ISBN 978-0-9995519-0-5

Library of Congress Control Number 2017916853

Names: Jardine, Jeff
Title: Home to the Brave : Remembrances of war brought home to one
small dot on a map
Subjects: World War II, Korea, Vietnam, Iraq, Afghanistan, Gulf War,
United States Army, Navy, Air Force, Marines, Northern San Joaquin
Valley, Modesto, California.

To Ernie, Milton, Jimmy, Arnie and so many others
who fought
to protect our freedoms

Contents

Introduction

During my 14 years as The Modesto Bee's columnist, I wrote more than five dozen columns about military veterans who shared their stories, their experiences and their post-war lives. These people and the times fascinated me, and still do.

Some unleashed emotions they'd kept locked away for decades.

Some told me stories that were more about humanity and humility than hostilities.

Some told me stories of heartbreak and sorrows.

And some described scars of war that still haunt them today, or did until the day they died.

My job? Simply to get out of their way and let them tell their stories.

Thus, I've assembled this collection of columns, the majority involving World War II but also from the Korean War, Cold War, Vietnam and Gulf wars.

What distinguishes these columns among countless other pieces written about wars or the military?

Only that each person in them lived or still lives within a small dot on the map of the United States: Stanislaus and surrounding counties in Northern California.

Their stories transcend state lines and regions. Modern military forces blend men and women from cities and towns spanning the entire nation. When their service ends, a soldier from Ceres might count another from New York City, a small town in Iowa, or anywhere else in the United States as his or her best friend and comrade in arms.

Consequently, you could plop a finger down just about anywhere on a map of the U.S., and veterans from there could share similar experiences or relate to the ones you'll read here. They might even have been involved directly or indirectly in these same stories.

I also wanted to bring the war home in ways that traditional combat stories could not. I wrote about how folks in Modesto – a town of about 25,000 in December 1941 – reacted to the news when they learned the Japanese had bombed Pearl Harbor that Sunday.

The monument in front of the Stanislaus County Courthouse contains the name of Modesto's only Pearl Harbor bombing casualty. Who was he though? That became one of my favorite columns ("Tale told for Modesto killed at Pearl Harbor.")

And yes, the table of contents is a bit top heavy with Pearl Harbor columns. It was a day, as President Franklin D. Roosevelt so eloquently stated, that lived in infamy. It needed to be remembered annually, both on the calendar and told by those who lived through it.

But you'll also read about Leroy Myers, a Modesto man whose imprisonment in Japan mirrored that of Louis Zamperini, whose story author Laura Hillenbrand told so poignantly in her book "Unbroken." As this went to print, Myers continues to live in Modesto and write poetry.

You'll read about the dreaded "missing in action" telegrams so often followed a month later by the messages of death.

You'll read about two men who, after moving into the same assisted living facility several years ago, discovered they'd both been POWs in the same prison in Hungary, just four floors apart at the exact same time.

You'll read about Bill Bahr, entrusted as a 22-year-old to escort bodies home for burial following World War II, and the impact it had on him so many years later.

You'll read about two valley women who flew military planes across the U.S. and were honored decades later by President Obama.

You'll read about a man who violated military protocol by flying a refueling plane more than 100 miles into North Vietnamese airspace to keep a shot-up F-4 plane from going down and its pilot from joining John McCain in the Hanoi Hilton – and how these two men finally met 43 years later.

And many, many more.

Ultimately, I wanted to do this book so that their stories would be bound together not unlike the men and women who fought throughout the various wars. I didn't want the columns to vanish into cyberspace or be buried on microfilm as the newspaper industry completes its transition away from print to online.

Sadly, but not unexpectedly, many of the people I profiled or interviewed for these columns from World War II are now gone, including three who passed during the time I compiled this book. In fact, according to the National World War II Museum in New Orleans, La., only 558,000 of the 16 million who served during World War II are still with us.

So many other stories will go untold.

I hope the columns move or fascinate you as much as they did me when I interviewed these heroes.

Jeff Jardine

Like so many other newspapers, The Modesto Bee produced extra editions on Dec. 7, 1941.

Edition after edition, Pearl Harbor story told

December 7, 2008

Any other day of the week, the sight of a paperboy hawking copies on Modesto's streets would have seemed perfectly normal.

But this was Sunday -- Dec. 7, 1941, to be precise. The Modesto Bee and News- Herald, as the paper was called then, didn't publish Sunday editions. So Modestans knew it had to be an extra, and newspapers usually print extras only when something really major -- and usually bad -- happened.

This one was bad beyond belief. Japan's attack on Pearl Harbor stunned America to its core, shattering the security its citizens had enjoyed for decades and plunging the nation into war. Until then, nowhere seemed safer and more secure than small-town America. Modesto had just 17,000 residents at the time, including the families of some soldiers and sailors stationed in Hawaii.

The nation's innocence ended the moment Americans heard of the attack over the radio or plopped down a nickel for a copy of the extras published that day.

Information wasn't instantly available, as it is today. The Bee published two and possibly three extras Dec. 7, producing the editions in small numbers because new information made them obsolete every few hours.

The paper, normally an afternoon publication, also published an extra on the morning of Dec. 8.

"My most vivid recollection was that The Modesto Bee put out an extra edition and the paperboy was walking down our street," said Betty Schroder, a former Bee reporter who lived on Elmwood Avenue at the time. "I was pretty shaken up. We were all pretty upset."

Out in Oakdale, enterprising 12-year-old paperboy Clayton Coleman figured the best place to sell papers that day was at the Oakdale rodeo grounds, which in 1941 were well outside town.

One of two Bee carriers in Oakdale (population 1,500), he said he outsold the town's other paperboy 4-to-1 by catching the eyes of motorists returning from the foothills on Highway 108-120.

The devastating attack -- and the vulnerability it exposed -- sent Americans across the country into a panic. They immediately went to lights-out conditions at night, valley residents included.

"We couldn't imagine anybody could be so stealthy and get away with it," said Bette Belle Smith, who was 20 at the time and heard the news over the radio.

Later, when she saw the now-famous photo of two Japanese envoys smiling as they left the State Department building in Washington, D.C., it all made sense.

"They knew Pearl Harbor was going to get bombed," Smith said.

Actually, the attack had occurred when the photo was taken. Word simply hadn't reached the mainland. Families of those serving in Hawaii had no way of knowing whether their loved ones had survived.

"Mom and Dad, they didn't know what to do," said Charles Streeter, 91, who served on the battleship USS California, which was damaged so heavily that it didn't return to duty until 1944. "They prayed and they hoped."

A day or so after the attack, the military handed out "v-mails," which were fold-over postcards the troops could send home. The sailor or soldier indicated on the card whether he'd been injured, Streeter said. They began arriving home about three days later.

"Mine said, 'I'm uninjured,' " he said.

With the California out of commission, Streeter moved to the heavy cruiser USS Chicago, which the Japanese torpedoed in January 1943. This time, he got a note to his parents through a friend who was returning to the mainland.

Peter Johansen, a former Modesto mayor, remembers returning from a day of skiing at Badger Pass in Yosemite National Park when he heard radio reports of the Pearl Harbor attack.

Johansen, who grew up east of Modesto, passed through town on his way back to San Francisco, where he lived at the time.

"As I drove into San Francisco, the streetcars weren't running," he said. "It was dark and there was a silence all over town. A scary night because, of course, San Francisco was a great place to attack."

He immediately enlisted in the Army Air Forces, but was rejected because of a rapid heartbeat.

"I went back to my job with my head hanging," Johansen said. "They'd given me a big send-off party and now I'm One-F."

Two years later, though, he was drafted into the same branch of the service.

"They weren't so picky that time," Johansen said.

Meanwhile, Smith remembers hearing President Franklin D. Roosevelt's "Day of Infamy" speech on the radio.

"We were all glued to it," she said.

Since then, Dec. 7, 1941, has maintained its place in America's collective heart as well as its craw. The San Joaquin Valley Chapter 10 of the Pearl Harbor Survivors Association is dwindling as its members die, along with so many others of their generation. That includes Coleman, The Bee's paperboy in Oakdale in 1941, who died of a heart attack last month at 79.

The Survivors Association's October meeting drew five members, said Evelyn Watts, the group's secretary. Her husband, Pearl Harbor survivor Virgil Watts, died in 2006.

There are other survivors from the valley who choose not to join. Many have told their stories -- of the explosions, the death, the danger, fire smoke and oil.

The fear at home was a different kind: the fear of the unknown.

The irony is that 67 years later, when we searched for copies of the Pearl Harbor Day extra edition, we found none here at The Bee -- not in our morgue (where originals are stored) or on microfilm.

Perhaps they were all sold at the time. Fortunately, retired Bee editor Ray

Nish had a couple of editions and loaned them to us.
Extra extras after all.

Tale told for Modestan killed at Pearl Harbor

December 6, 2011

It's a window into history, the Dec. 12, 1941, story in The Bee telling of the area's first serviceman killed in World War II action.

"Modesto Youth Is War Casualty" read the headline below the photo of a smiling J.B. Delane Miller.

Five days before -- 70 years ago tomorrow -- the Japanese attacked Pearl Harbor. Reading that five-paragraph story today, I found it intriguing by what it didn't reveal. The story didn't specify that Miller, 23, died during the actual attack, which wasn't all that surprising.

A day or so after Pearl Harbor, the government announced it would not immediately release names of those killed in the attack, fearing the information might help the enemy.

Debbie Noda / The Modesto Bee

Marjorie Miller, with photo and documents of her brother-in-law, J.B. Delane Miller.

In fact, the name of his ship -- the USS Tennessee --- embroidered on the front of his Navy cap had been blacked out for the photo released to the newspaper. Family members were discouraged from revealing much of what they knew.

No story detailed Miller's all-too short life. Did he grow up in Modesto? Attend local schools?

Amid the immediate hysteria of the war, and with local men enlisting by the dozens, Miller's death didn't get the same kind of coverage those who subsequently died in Iraq or Afghanistan received. He was buried in Honolulu. His family, it seems, held no memorial service for him in Modesto.

Like so many others at the time, Miller's story quickly dissolved into the background, held only in the hearts of those who knew and loved him.

Who was he? His parents, brother and two sisters all are deceased. So my Nov. 29 column included a note asking any surviving kin or friends to contact me, not really expecting to get a response.

Late last week, Marjorie Miller of Modesto called. Her late husband, Theo Miller, was J.B.'s younger brother and there are numerous other relatives in the area, though most were born after J.B. died. In fact, she owns an album containing photos, letters and official military correspondence regarding J.B. Her memorabilia includes the last letter he wrote to his parents and his death notice from the Navy Department via Postal Telegraph, a Western Union competitor of the day.

Marjorie, who knew him in Oklahoma before marrying his brother and later moving west, filled in the details of J.B.'s life. (J.B., by the way, stood for John Bert).

He was born March 24, 1918, in Oklahoma. He graduated in 1937 from Gould High — where he was voted "most handsome" — in Harmon County, Okla., on the Texas border. Dust Bowl migrants, his parents came to the Central Valley in the mid-1930s and eventually settled into a house at 1209 S. 10th St., south of Modesto.

J.B., though, remained in Oklahoma to attend junior college and lived with the family of his cousin, Clarence Miller.

"He was a really neat guy," said Clarence Miller, now of San Diego. "Everybody liked him. The last picture I saw of him, he was in Long Beach and he sent a picture of him and his girlfriend (circa 1939). He was about 10 years older (than Clarence). I wish I could have known him longer."

J.B. Miller eventually joined his family in Modesto for a brief time before enlisting in the Navy in 1939, and his parents' address became his own. In that manner, he became a Modestan — hence the only one known to have died in the Pearl Harbor attack.

"He was a very energetic fellow," Marjorie remembers. "A lot of fun to be around. He was a really nice brother-in-law."

In one letter home, he wrote that he hoped to be home for Christmas. But the Navy and particularly Hawaii, she said, became his real home.

"(I'd) stay here the rest of my life before I'd pick another bale of cotton," J.B. wrote.

One of J.B.'s letters noted a visit from brother Theo, who was heading home to be discharged from the Navy. Their visit happened Dec. 2, five days before the attack and the day Theo had reached San Francisco to muster out. Already married to Marjorie, Theo went on to Oklahoma to reunite with his wife.

Over the years, Theo and Marjorie talked often about J.B., but never about how he might have died.

"(Theo) didn't talk about it," she said.

The Navy didn't offer details and the family didn't pursue them. Now, of course, information is available on the Internet. Records show J.B. Delane Miller served on the USS Tennessee, moored alongside the USS West Virginia when the Japanese attacked. Of the two bombs that struck the ship, one hit a gun turret. It failed to explode but broke apart. Fragments of the bomb and one of the gun barrels, according to survivors' accounts, killed three of the five USS Tennessee crewmen who died that day.

J.B. likely died at that time, Marjorie Miller said.

"We were told J.B. was there when a bomb was dropped on the deck," she said. "It didn't explode, but the concussion got him."

A satellite now pinpoints his gravestone at the National Cemetery Memorial of the Pacific in Honolulu.

Likewise, seven decades later, J.B. Delane Miller is among the names etched in stone on the monument in downtown's courthouse park, listing Stanislaus County residents who died in World War I and subsequent wars.

It doesn't say when or where he died. It doesn't tell you he was the only known Modesto resident, however tenuous the connection, killed at Pearl Harbor.

It represents a story that, like all the rest, deserved to be told.

65 years later, Pearl Harbor still vivid

December 7, 2006

Fred McMullen suppressed the memories for decades.

His family knew he had survived Japan's attack on Pearl Harbor 65 years ago today. The Gustine man, now 87, told a few stories over the years, but spared them the gruesome details.

"Not ever," said his wife, Betty. "He just never talked about it. He was always quiet about it."

Debbie Noda / The Modesto Bee
Fred McMullen kept his Pearl Harbor attack memories from his family for decades.

Then, in 2002, their family surprised the couple with a Hawaiian vacation for their 50th wedding anniversary. It was the first time he'd returned since the "date which will live in infamy," as President Franklin D. Roosevelt called it.

Their trip coincided with a reunion that included seven other survivors from his ship, the USS Nevada, and memorial ceremonies for those killed on the Nevada and the USS Oklahoma. And he visited the USS Arizona memorial.

The sounds, the acrid smoke, the smells, the horrors -- they all came back that day.

"It was emotional," McMullen said. "I'd never talked to my kids about it, or very much, until I got back. Then I started."

"After he went, we've heard all about it," Betty said.

Fred McMullen is among the dwindling number of Pearl Harbor survivors in the Northern San Joaquin Valley. He is a real find, since he's never belonged to the valley's survivors' association, which lost four members in 2006.

McMullen enlisted in the Navy in 1940, getting 16 weeks of boot camp before being assigned to the Nevada. The ship had just completed a patrol south of Guam before heading back to Pearl Harbor and mooring behind the Arizona.

The morning of Dec. 7, the Nevada prepared to send a small motorboat carrying a coxswain and two others from Battleship Row to Oahu.

"About that time, the (Japanese) planes came over Ford Island," McMullen said. "It was no drill. It was the real thing."

The other two men in the small boat were ordered back to the Nevada while the coxswain went toward the main island alone, McMullen said.

"He never made it back," he said. "I remember the strafing really well. They emptied all of their machine guns before they returned to their ship to lighten their load."

One plane, McMullen said, returned to attack three times.

"We lost about 35 men on the upper deck because their tracers ignited our ready-service ammo," he said.

The Nevada took one torpedo and several bomb hits. The ship ran aground, afire, while trying to escape the harbor.

When one plane came over low, McMullen went on the attack. "I threw a marlinespike (splicing tool) at him out of frustration," he said. "I don't know if I hit him or not."

As the strafing and bombing raged, McMullen saw two officers fall right next to him, hit by bullets. And the explosions from the ammo on the deck caused more damage.

"We had lots of powder burns," he said. "You could reach over and touch a guy by the shoulder and it was like roasted pork -just mushy."

Caught by surprise once, they weren't about to let it happen again. The evening of Dec. 7, a couple of American planes flew over the Army's Schofield Barracks without their running lights on.

"We fired our broadside gun on Schofield Barracks," McMullen said.

With the Nevada needing serious repairs - it was out of commission until February 1942 - McMullen was assigned to the light cruiser St. Louis the day after the Pearl Harbor attack.

"We went out to sea to see if we could find the Japanese fleet," McMullen said. "We didn't find 'em."

He spent the remainder of the war on the St. Louis and left the Navy in 1948, having earned a Bronze Star, a president's unit citation, a Navy citation and 20 war stripes. Two years later, living in Santa Rosa, N.M., his trailer caught fire and all his remnants of the war were destroyed -- all except the images etched in his memory. Those surfaced occasionally in the form of nightmares, his wife said.

McMullen spent 15 years in heavy construction, helping to build the San Luis Reservoir Dam, Interstate 5 and the California Aqueduct before going into farming "and falling flat on my face," he said.

It wasn't until after the 2002 trip that he began opening up to his family about his war experiences in great detail. He also decided the medals and documents were worth having, and Betty contacted Veterans Affairs officials to start the process.

McMullen received the replacements at Christmastime 2004, just days before he and Betty celebrated their 52nd wedding anniversary.

Retired just two years ago, he regularly attends ceremonies at the San Joaquin Valley National Cemetery in Santa Nella. But he's never been involved in the Pearl Harbor Survivors' Association or any veterans group.

"I didn't join anything," McMullen said.

That's not surprising to those who know him.

His memories of the attack on Pearl Harbor were his own for 61 years. It took a return trip to Pearl Harbor, a gift from his family four years ago, to unlock them.

Fred McMullen died at 88 in 2008.

Infamous day's witnesses wane

December 6, 2012

On a hill overlooking Pearl Harbor, Ken Krause played with the landlord's dogs.

Just shy of 3 years old, he couldn't possibly begin to understand the magnitude of what was happening below as Japanese planes attacked on the morning of Dec. 7, 1941.

"All I remember was the planes flying over," said Krause, a longtime Oakdale resident, now 73.

OK, he recalls a bit more, such as the Hawaiian couple who lived in the basement of the home that Krause's mom and sailor father rented. The landlords spoke the native tongue, and their attempts in English involved heavy pidgin at best. Presumably, they wanted him to go inside the house.

"Hawaiian was like a foreign language," he

Debbie Noda / The Modesto Bee
Ken Krause watched planes bomb Pearl Harbor from a hill top away from the Navy base as a 3-year-old in 1941.

said. "They were waving at me to do something. I couldn't understand them at all. What they wanted me to do, I had no idea."

And he remembers that his mother, Helen, was four months pregnant with his sister and in bed that morning.

"She was looking at a mirror that reflected toward Pearl Harbor, and she could not comprehend what she was seeing," Krause said.

Within a few years, it likely will fall to Krause to serve as the valley's resident eyewitness to the moment that changed the world forever. Membership in the valley's Pearl Harbor survivors' associations, which numbered about 100 in 2000, has dwindled to two after Leon Pitts of Merced died at 89 in April. Only 88-year-old Robert Fernandez of Stockton and 96-year-old John Smith of Waterford remain, though there might be other Pearl survivors still living who, for whatever reasons, never joined any of the organizations.

Krause was born at Mare Island in Vallejo, where his father, chief signalman Edward Krause, served before moving the family to Hawaii. He had been assigned to the USS Minneapolis, based at Pearl Harbor with the rest of the fleet, months before the attack.

Courtesy of Ken Krause

Edward Krause and son Ken in Hawaii well before the attack.

On Dec. 7, the heavy cruiser steamed eight miles out to sea to fire its big guns for the filming of a movie titled "To the Shores of Tripoli." Otherwise, the Minneapolis would have been moored near battleship row and a target of the Japanese planes.

Edward Krause kept detailed notes of the attack in a log his son still reads and cherishes.

" ... all of a sudden, we observed hundreds of AA (anti-aircraft) shells bursting in one area directly over Pearl Harbor, water spurts and spouts could be seen," Edward Krause wrote. "I've actually seen two bombs drop, soon a belch of black thick smoke rose then continued for some time."

Entries include reports he heard over KGU, a Honolulu radio station:

" 'Urgent, urgent, this is no drill, Pearl Harbor, Hickam Field and Wheeler Field attack by aircraft.' "

The elder Krause noted that many crewmen believed it was a drill until the ship received an official dispatch that read, "attacking planes have red circle under wings, believe to be Japanese," and he made entries every few minutes or so.

After the attack, the USS Minneapolis patrolled for Japanese submarines until returning to Pearl on Dec. 10, at which time Edward Krause logged vivid descriptions of the death and damage, the sunken battleships and other warships.

"He documented it really well," Ken Krause said.

While dad received orders to ship out again, mom got hers as well.

"She was told to pack everything in boxes and be ready to leave on a moment's notice," Ken Krause said. "We lived out of boxes until the middle of February (1942). They put us aboard the Lurline (a liner) and sent us back to Oakland. I remember looking out of the porthole and seeing a tin-can destroyer escorting us back to the West Coast."

They lived in the East Bay throughout the war while dad fought in the Pacific.

As so often happens in life, things have a way of coming full circle, and Krause's story is no exception. He returned to Pearl Harbor in the spring of 1959, nearly 18 years after the attack, and this time as a Navy man instead of a toddler.

"I was on the nuclear sub Swordfish, the first nuclear sub to have Pearl Harbor as a home port," Krause said. "They were celebrating statehood."

Remnants of the attack remained then and still do today, in wreckage and emotions.

"I had a bumper sticker made for my wife's car," Krause said. " 'If there hadn't been a Pearl Harbor, there wouldn't have been a Hiroshima.' "

For most everyone else, Dec. 7, 1941, is an annual remembrance. To Krause, it is part of his fabric. San Joaquin Valley Chapter 10 of the Pearl Harbor Association still meets every other month at a restaurant in Modesto. Krause is an associate member. Full membership is limited to those who were in the military and on the island during the attack. He attends the meetings out of respect to his father and to the remaining survivors.

"I go to support the guys that served," Krause said. "Fellows who were there still carry the terrible things that happened. They lost a lot of shipmates who were friends. It never goes away."

They do, though, and one day in the not-too-distant future, Krause could be left as the valley's last living link to the day that changed the world.

Ken Krause lives in Oakdale with wife Millie.

Veteran 'lucky' his ship didn't come in

December 6, 2009

You might say Warren Brown survived the attack on Pearl Harbor because he went to the movies.

Or, perhaps more accurately, because the movies came to him.

Either way, he was a Navy electrician aboard the USS Minneapolis on Dec. 7, 1941. The heavy cruiser conducted gunnery practice a couple of miles offshore for the benefit of filmmakers when the Japanese attacked the American Fleet.

"We were just a short ways out to sea with some Hollywood producers aboard," the 88-year-old Modestan said. "They were filming us firing our eight-inch guns at a target. I think the movie was 'The Shores of Tripoli,' and Martha Raye was in it."

He was close on the movie title, though not on its star. "To the Shores of Tripoli" premièred in 1942, headlined by John Payne (not Wayne), Maureen O'Hara and Randolph Scott. None of the actors set foot on the Minneapolis, Brown said. A camera crew and directors gathered big-gun footage to use in the film later described by some critics as an unabashed flag-waving recruitment piece for the Marine Corps.

There are three constants among Pearl Harbor survivors. First and most obvious, they survived. Second, most in their late 80s or early 90s, and are dwindling in numbers along with the rest of the World War II veterans. And third, they have unique stories of where they were, what they did and how the events of that day affected them.

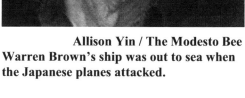

Allison Yin / The Modesto Bee
Warren Brown's ship was out to sea when the Japanese planes attacked.

Some escaped bombed-out ships, the horrible smell of burning oil and death etched in their memories forever.

Others remember trying to fight back, as futile as it might seem now.

Then there are those like Brown, a man of incredible good fortune who happened to be out of harm's way during the Pearl Harbor attack and lived to survive the battles at Coral Sea, Midway and in the Philippines as well.

"I saw a lot," he said. "(My ships) didn't get hit a lot. I feel lucky for that."

Beginning with the infamous attack 68 years ago Monday.

"I'd just had breakfast – 'chow,' we called it -- and I went out to sit on the bow," Brown said. "I looked over at Pearl Harbor and saw the smoke. It wasn't very long before they sounded general quarters."

The Japanese pilots ignored the Minneapolis along with the three destroyers and tugboat off in the distance to concentrate on pounding Battleship Row and anything else in the harbor, including ships the Minneapolis would have been moored alongside had it not been on the filming mission.

As the attack ended, the Minneapolis went out to hunt for Japanese submarines. He didn't see the devastation at Pearl Harbor for about a week, the movie crew with them the entire time.

"There was oil everywhere in the harbor," Brown said. "All the battleships were sunk. It was horrible."

The Minneapolis crew months later plucked hundreds of survivors from the water after the Japanese bombed the carrier USS Lexington into a flaming carcass at the Battle of the Coral Sea in 1942.

Lucky? Later that year, Japanese planes bore down on the cluster of American ships that included the Minneapolis.

Courtesy of Warren Brown
Warren Brown during his Navy days.

"They were strafing our ships, and I started running for the bow, although that probably wasn't the best idea," Brown said. "There were 85,000 gallons of high-octane gas up there. One of their planes flew over our bow only about eight to nine feet above us and hit the LSD (docked landing ship) next to us and blew it to smithereens. I don't know why it didn't hit us."

Brown stayed with the Minneapolis through the Midway and Guadalcanal battles before returning to the States to commission a seaplane tender in Bremerton, Wash., early in 1943. He made it through the rest of the war safe and sound only to be assigned to monitor the atomic bomb testing at the Bikini Atoll in 1946. His ship, the USS Hughes, served as one of the testing targets. He and other Hughes crewmen boarded other ships and steamed several miles away to witness the explosions.

Anchored away from the immediate blast area, the Hughes still felt the impacts of the bomb that scuttled the venerable carrier USS Saratoga. Weeks after the test, the military sent him back to the ship -- Geiger counter in hand to monitor the radiation -- to see if he could get the Hughes operational again.

"That Geiger counter was just screaming," he said. "I had to take two or three showers" (to reduce his own radiation levels).

Yet he never experienced any of the ill effects usually associated with radiation exposure. In fact, he lost two wives to lung cancer before he himself developed prostate cancer in 1994.

His treatment?

"Radiation," Brown said. "It got rid of it. No more cancer."

He enjoyed a long career as a union electrician in Modesto before retiring in 1981, and maintains his union membership.

Brown finally quit riding his motorcycle a few years ago, but still rides a motorized scooter or a bicycle when he isn't driving.

"I can still get around pretty well," he said. "I'm in pretty good shape for 88."

He's indeed a man whose seemingly endless lucky streak began when his ship served as a movie extra that fateful day in December 1941.

And what did Brown think of "To the Shores of Tripoli"?

"I never saw that movie," he said.

He didn't need to. He'd already survived it.

Warren Brown died at 93 in 2015.

A once busy sky

WWII fighter, bomber crews trained locally

March 31, 2003

The fields and orchards of western Stanislaus County are a study in silence, broken only by an occasional gust of wind or a truck rumbling down a country road.

But for more than two years in the 1940s, the skies of the West Side moaned with the twin engines of bombers and high-pitched whine of Hellcat fighter planes.

World War II came to the valley in a big way when the Navy hastily built bases at tiny enclaves such as Vernalis and Crows Landing. Hundreds of pilots trained at the bases, 18 miles apart and tucked against the Coast Ranges. Thousands more worked as crew, servicing the planes, guarding prisoners and doing their part for the war effort.

Yet today, few people know the freestanding concrete wall in Vernalis is the last vestige of a prisoner-of-war camp.

Few travelers along Interstate 5, who see huge piles of compost and farm products, could possibly know they're looking at the runway of an abandoned Navy airfield. But make no mistake about it: These airfields -- and those who trained there -- became part of the valley's wartime fabric.

The day after the mind-numbing attack on Pearl Harbor was perhaps the most predictable in American history.

"December 8, 1941. Everybody went down to sign up," said Hughson's Dave Orth, then a 19-year-old studying at Modesto Junior College. "President Roosevelt told all us young guys to cool it. Go back and finish your schooling."

America, having just endured the Great Depression, seemed as unprepared for war as it was for the Japanese attack.

INSTANT AIR BASES

It needed time to build the factories to build the ships, planes and tanks, and the guns, bombs, shells and bullets needed for war. It needed places to train the soldiers, sailors and aviators.

It didn't take long. By the time Orth enlisted in the Army in 1942, Merced Army Air Field -- which later became Castle Air Force Base -- had opened. Also, the Army Air Corps began operations at Stockton Field, where Orth spent 21 months as a crew chief before shipping to China. The Army added fields at Tracy, New Jerusalem southeast of Tracy, and at Sharpe Army Depot in Lathrop.

The Navy needed only about six months to build the Crows Landing and Vernalis naval auxiliary air stations, commissioning them 15 days apart in spring 1943. The Crows Landing base became home to aircraft carrier squadrons, 268 officers and 2,116 enlisted men. By comparison, the town of Crows Landing had a population of about 370, one gas station and a freight train stop.

The Navy built the Vernalis base north of Gaffery Road on 700 acres it purchased for $25,000. It constructed a 7,000-foot-long asphalt runway and a tarmac, and quickly added barracks, hangars, offices and a 400-meter oval track.

"The day they came in here, they flew over, and a few hours later they had equipment working," said Ray Murphy, 74, whose family sold part of the land for the base. He was a young boy then on the family ranch, where he still lives, south of the airfield. At the time, Vernalis had a country store that doubled as the post office, and little else.

The base was built to handle multi-engine patrol squadrons, including bombers. The Navy quickly decided that the planes were better suited for the thicker concrete runways at Crows Landing. So the bases swapped duties, with the bombers going to Crows Landing and the carrier planes training at Vernalis.

CLOSE ONLY IN PROXIMITY

Both bases were part of Alameda Naval Air Station and were just 18 miles apart, yet they had only occasional contact, said Modesto resident Clinton Ray, a member of the first squadron at Crows Landing in 1943.

"We were pretty much separate," Ray said. "We never got together and played any ball games with them or anything. But we did have one of our pilots mistakenly land at Vernalis."

A phone call let the Crows Landing staff know their pilot wasn't hurt or missing -- just embarrassed.

"By the time he got back to Crows Landing, we had made a big sign: 'Welcome Home!' " Ray said.

Each afternoon, a plane from Alameda brought in personnel, aircraft parts and mail. Modesto's Phil Marquart spent time at both bases, moving to Crows Landing with the bombers in 1944 and staying until it closed in 1946. While there, he endured the Battle of Patterson.

"We'd put out a circle of flares for bombing practice at night," Marquart said. Pilots practiced by dropping small cast-iron bombs that were about 10 inches long, each with a shotgun shell in the tip. When the bomb landed, the shell exploded, creating a flash and white smoke to tell the pilot where it had landed.

"One of the pilots got confused," Marquart said.

There also is a circle of lights in downtown Patterson, where the city's well-known traffic circle is the hub of its wheel-shaped street pattern.

"He dropped two bombs," Marquart said. "One of them, I think, hit a hairdresser's (salon) and the other hit the police station."

Fortunately, it was after 5 p.m., and the town had closed up for the night.

"A direct hit would probably have killed somebody," he said.

And there were tragedies, such as the one that Lester Stein of Grayson witnessed when a pilot died about a mile from his family's farm.

"I was milking cows outside one day, and (a plane) crashed over here on Faust Road," Stein said. "The plane ... came straight down."

A CREWMAN'S LIFE

John Mount arrived at Crows Landing from San Diego's Camp Kearney in 1944 as a sheet metal specialist assigned to work on low-altitude bombers.

"It was hot in August, and our planes weren't here yet," he said. "So they told us to take a 72-hour liberty and then come back. The planes weren't there when we got back, so they told us to take another 72-hour liberty. We took three of those before the planes arrived, but once they came in, that didn't happen anymore."

Crews treasured their liberties because of the increased workloads as Allies looked to defeat the Germans and turn their efforts against the Japanese. When he got one, Mount headed for Modesto, and it did not take long to empty his pockets.

"They'd send us out on a liberty and we'd spend all of our money right away," said Mount, who has lived in Ceres since the war ended. "It didn't take long to go through $78 a month in pay."

So Mount, like many Navy crewmen, found part-time jobs to earn extra cash.

"I worked in the canneries," he said. "They'd hire you whether they needed you or not."

Mount went to the theaters, bars and restaurants in Modesto, catching rides on cattle trucks running between Crows Landing and Modesto. The bases also ran buses each day to Modesto and Patterson.

"The people in Modesto were just wonderful," said Mount, who met his wife in the valley. "You'd be standing around talking, and someone would come up to you and start talking. After a while, they'd say, '...How'd you like to come over for a chicken dinner?' They just took care of the boys. What a good bunch of people out here."

Others went to Patterson, where they could swim at the high school pool, or to Newman, where a contingent of pretty Portuguese girls caught the aviators' eyes, Mount said.

REMNANTS

When the war ended in 1945, so did Vernalis' days as an air base. Jazz legend Louis Armstrong and his band played at the Harvest Ball at the base days before the Navy deactivated the field. Three months later -- and 18 months after the base was commissioned -- the Navy left. A German prisoner-of-war camp, along Welty Road near Highway 132, outlasted the air base. POWs earned 80 cents a day working on farms in the area and also built the Olympic-size pool at the Vernalis base.

The POW camp closed in 1946, when the last of the Germans went home. All that remains is a 12-foot high concrete wall where the prisoners played handball.

Jim Davis, owner of Sun Dry Products, now owns the base. He uses runways to dry various materials and ag products. He leases part of the facility to Grover Landscaping Services, which grinds and dries compost there.

"Every once in a while -- maybe once a year – we'll have someone stop by who was here during the war," Davis said. "They just want to see it again."

Many buildings still stand, including the old brig, which Davis uses for storage. The compass rose -- a round slab of concrete where planes checked the accuracy of their compasses -- also remains.

Crows Landing Naval Auxiliary Air Station was decommissioned July 6, 1946, but was used in various ways until 1996. The Navy turned the Crows

Landing airfield over to the National Aeronautics and Space Administration in 1994, but remains responsible for environmental cleanup of the base. Most of the buildings have been demolished. This summer, Stanislaus County hopes to receive the deed to the base and begin converting it into a business-air park. So it might again have a future as an aviation center.

But don't underestimate what these quiet fields in the valley did for the country during World War II, said Mount, the former bomber maintenance crewman at Crows Landing.

"We did our part."

The base now belongs to Stanislaus County. A major development plan fell apart in 2012, and the county continues consider uses for the base.

Navy vet survived torpedo, escaped flashbacks

May 24, 2009

For one panic-stricken moment off the coast of Italy nearly 66 years ago, it seemed a tossup whether Robert Abbott would live to someday be honored as veteran or remembered among those who died in war.

His ship, the destroyer USS Rowan (DD-405), headed to the bottom after taking a torpedo hit from a German E-boat. The suction pulled Abbott down with the ship, which sank in just over one minute. The 86-year-old Turlock resident can only guess how long he stayed under water, how deep he went or why the sinking ship's insistent pull suddenly let him go. He only knows that he had held his breath so long that his lungs felt as if they were about to explode before he could scramble to the surface.

Abbott knows he and 69 others lived and 204 of their crew mates died shortly after midnight on Sept. 11, 1943. Many who survived World War II kept the horrors to themselves, never telling even their wives and children what they experienced. Only in recent years have some broken their silence about seeing so much death and losing friends. Yet others can't contain their emotions on Memorial Day, D-Day, Pearl Harbor Day or other days of remembrance.

Brian Ramsay / The Modesto Bee
Robert Abbott survived U-boat torpedo.

Abbott, though, feels lucky in two respects. First, he survived that horrific day and later served in the Pacific campaign at Okinawa. Second, because of the way the Rowan went down and the injuries Abbott suffered, he never saw any of his shipmates die. Consequently, he's never endured the flashbacks or the feelings that affected some other war survivors.

"I just don't think about it much, actually," Abbott said. "It probably would be different if I saw lots of bodies."

By September 1943, 19-year-old Abbott had been in the Navy for a year. On Sept. 11, a few minutes after midnight, he strapped himself into his 20mm gun station down behind the Rowan's conning tower. While cruising the Mediterranean on its way to the Algerian port city of Oran, the Benham-class destroyer encountered the German E-boat -- a bigger, faster version of the American sub chaser. The Germans owned the edge in maneuverability.

"We were running away, firing our 5½-inch guns at 'em," Abbott said. "The old man (Lt. Cmdr. Robert Ford) decided he wasn't going to run anymore."

Ford ordered the ship repositioned for a better shot -- the wrong call, as it turned out.

"We turned right into a torpedo," Abbott said.

The torpedo hit near the rear engine room, triggering a massive explosion.

"It probably hit a powder magazine," he said.

The blast slammed Abbott's head into the gun's sight. The impact left him bloodied, bruised and dazed. It shattered his eardrums and he briefly lost consciousness. Though in pain, he quickly came to and unhooked himself from the gun station as the ship began to sink.

"Right away, I had water up to my knees, and the next thing I knew, I was under water," he said.

Ultimately, that dreaded midnight watch became a big part of the reason he survived. Most of the 204 who died were sleeping below and never had a chance when the torpedo hit. They died instantly or drowned, trapped inside the ship as it went down. When the suction finally released Abbott to the surface, he heard sailors' voices in a life raft.

"I hung on to that," he said.

Maybe an hour later, crewmen from a small boat pulled him -- so stiff and sore that he couldn't move -- out of the water and took him to the destroyer USS Bristol.

"I was black and blue, and my clothes were all ripped," he said. "We found out later that there were 10 men up there (in the gunnery position on the Rowan) and only three of us got off."

He spent weeks healing in a Naval hospital stateside, taking a permanent souvenir back with him into active duty.

"I've still got a piece of metal in my neck," he said.

Discharged from the Navy in 1947, Abbott came to the valley and worked repairing farm machinery.

For many years, he remained active in the USS Rowan survivors' group and attended his last reunion about 12 years ago. So few from the Rowan (DD-405) remained that they merged with crews from the fourth ship to bear the Rowan name, (DD-782).

"People were getting older and in ill health," Abbott said. "We couldn't continue on by ourselves."

Now, he and two others are the last of the USS Rowan (DD-405) survivors. Time has claimed the rest, with each passing noted in a survivors' newsletter. Though many veterans and those who lost loved ones in battle will spend Memorial Day remembering and reflecting, Abbott probably won't.

"I never saw lots of dead," Abbott said. "I'm probably pretty fortunate that way."

Abbott lives in Turlock

Dreaded telegram

Military tries to soften death's blow

November 9, 2003

Lois Hartley Hunter remembers June 1944 all too well.

Blue stars in the window of her family's home in Oakdale proudly told the world that two Hartley sons -- Jack and Howard -- were fighting for America. Just 14 years old at the time, Lois was visiting friends a couple of houses away one afternoon when a car stopped in front of her home.

Howard Hartley

Courtesy of Lois Hartley Hunter

She recognized the car and its driver -- possibly the town's postmaster, she now recalls. Then her dad got out of the car, too, and began a slow walk to the house. As she came running home, she saw that he carried a Western Union telegram. Two older brothers at war ... her dad's body language ... the telegram in hand. It all bore the mark of tragedy.

Howard's low-flying bomber had been shot down over France eight days after D-Day and he was missing, the telegram read. Had her brother been captured by the Germans and sent to a stalag? Or … ?

"You just had to have hope," Hunter said. "(The Germans) were taking prisoners. But when you're in a low-flying bomber and you get hit, there's not much chance."

Four months later, they received another telegram -- the one they dreaded most.

"Report now states he was killed in action fourteen July over France," it read.

Friends came by to help them grieve. The war went on with more death, more telegrams.

Fast forward to last week, when an Army officer came to the Lau family home in Livingston to tell them that their daughter, Karina, had been killed in Iraq. The Laus will be treated much differently than the Hartleys and other families who lost loved ones in World War II and Korea.

The military simply does a better job of consoling and assisting surviving family members than it did back then.

The Laus got the news within hours of their daughter's death, from an officer ordered to tell them before they saw it on a cable news station. Families would rather hear it from the mouth of another soldier than get a phone call or, worse yet, a slip of paper that begins "The War Department regrets to inform you ... ."

Even though telegrams were a frequent mode of communication in the 1940s and '50s, stomachs still knotted and faces turned grim whenever a Western Union or postal telegraph messenger boy went into a neighborhood to deliver one.

After the first wave of American casualties during the Vietnam War, the military began sending officers to break the news. It has been that way ever since. Now, Army Maj. Steve Stover said, officers are assigned specific responsibilities when a soldier dies in the line of duty.

The military reports all deaths and missing-in-actions to a casualty assessment unit and morgue in Alexandria, Va. Working off a list of notification officers available in each region of the country, the military sends one to the home within four hours after a death is confirmed. The notification officer meets only once with the family to break the bad news.

"The problem is that the family might resent him," Stover said.

Another officer is then assigned to the family, usually by the next day.

"He keeps the family up on entitlements and benefits, how to deal with the remains and (retrieving) personal property," Stover said. "And he keeps the family up on any information if there is an investigation."

By comparison, the Hartleys and so many other American families leaned on one another for support. Soon after Howard's death was confirmed, the family replaced his blue star with a gold one that signified that he had died for his country.

Mabel Hartley, Howard's mother, drew close to Mrs. Orvis, Mrs. Charlesworth, Mrs. Condrey and Mrs. Dorroh -- all Oakdale gold-star mothers who lost sons in the war.

"They formed a bond," Lois Hartley Hunter said.

Beyond receiving a letter of sympathy from an Army officer, the Hartleys had little other contact with the military beyond making arrangements to bring Howard's body home to be buried in the Oakdale cemetery.

War remains the same. Soldiers die. Families grieve.

It's just that the American military now tries to do a better job of easing their pain.

Adrian Mendoza / The Modesto Bee
Lois Hartley Hunter displays the telegrams that told of her brother's disappearance, then of his death.

Hunter lives in Hughson.

Rendering 'Final Salute' a solemn job

Veteran recalls his service as an escort for WWII military dead

May 30, 2010

Bill Bahr had seen plenty of death. He saw it in the Pacific campaign in the Navy as World War II came to its end.

He saw it again in the blistering cold of Korea, when he was in the Army.

But nothing, the 84-year-old valley resident said, jarred his soul like the death he experienced back home in the United States in between those two wars. For 23 months beginning in October 1947, he delivered America's World War II dead back to their families as a sergeant in the Army's Military Escort Service.

Bart Ah You / The Modesto Bee
Bill Bahr brought home heroes for burial as a military escort after World War II.

In charge of the casket bearing the remains of a young man killed in battle, Bahr bore the absolute duty of making sure the soldier went home to receive his proper military burial and his "final salute."

While many people in the United States today see Memorial Day as a three-day weekend to usher in the summer play season, Bahr experienced Memorial Day roughly 120 times over those two years. Each time, he became the face of the military to the grieving mothers, fathers, sisters and brothers. Some wanted answers he could not provide. Others took him into their homes as their own, as a temporary living stand-in for the son they'd lost.

Quite a burden, indeed -- even more so when you consider he was only 22 when he took his first soldier home.

"I was discharged from the Navy in 1946 and went back to Iowa," said Bahr, who now lives in Stockton and recently began visiting the Stanislaus Veterans Center in Modesto for post-traumatic stress disorder counseling. "I tried to find work, but there'd been too many servicemen released and not enough jobs."

Over beers with a friend one day, the buddy said he was about to go.

"I said, 'Where are you going?' " Bahr said. "He said, 'Back to the Army.' I thought about it, and I applied in Chicago."

After a brief training, he was promoted to sergeant and assigned to Fort Sheridan, about 35 miles north of Chicago. The military used the now-defunct base as its Midwest distribution center for bodies returning from World War II.

"It was gut-wrenching," he said. "My first day, they took me to a warehouse. It was about four blocks long by two blocks wide and two stories high. Not an inch of it didn't have a casket."

Assigned one casket at a time, Bahr received any available information about the dead soldier and how and where he died. Sometimes, he knew little more than the soldier's name, family and hometown. He carried total responsibility for the casket from the moment it left the distribution center until the end of the funeral. He coordinated the services with local funeral directors, but took orders from no one. In fact, Congress bestowed so much power upon the military escorts that "the only person who could supersede me was the president of the United States," Bahr said.

Most of the trips involved night-time train travel so he would arrive at the soldier's hometown in the morning.

"You wore black arm bands and white gloves," Bahr said. "People always knew who you were. You might be there for three days."

Some of the families latched onto the escorts as surrogate sons. They'd want the casket kept at their home until the funeral, and the soldier's mother would implore Bahr, mature beyond his years despite his boyish face, to stay in her son's room.

"You'd get to dwelling on it," Bahr said. "There's his baseball glove. Everything's just like he left it. You spend three days looking at his picture. The second day, they wanted a hug to remind them of the son they'd lost."

He always gave it, even though he was uncomfortable doing so.

"His mother would tell you what he liked for dinner," Bahr said. "His father would tell you what a great football player he'd been. And I'm thinking, 'Yeah, he was a great kid. But I've got to bury him.' Each time, I had to bury a friend. I'd think about the final salute you made at the end of the service. What a relief. ... But it wasn't over. You were still there with the family."

Some of the families understood that these young military escorts hurt, too. One southern Indiana family -- a very poor one -- touched him in a way he'll never forget.

"We didn't get much money (maybe $75 a month)," Bahr said. "That family didn't have anything. But as I left, the father ran up and handed me a handkerchief filled with coins. About $6 worth. They didn't have anything, yet they took up a collection for me. It really shakes you up."

Other families, however, weren't so hospitable. Bringing a solider home to Kentucky's hill country, Bahr once found himself arrested and placed in protective custody by the local sheriff.

"The boys in the hills are upset you're bringing bodies back," he said the sheriff told him. The local funeral director added, "You'd better stay on board (the train). Otherwise, they'll take a shot at you."

It was the only time, Bahr said, he didn't stay with the casket until burial. Other families took their frustrations out on Bahr verbally.

"In Kansas City, the funeral director met me at the train," Bahr said. "He told me, 'These people are very bitter.' His father said, 'You S.O.B. You're the bastard who killed my son.' I said to him, 'Here's your flag.' He said, 'I don't want that goddamned flag.' "

At that point, Bahr said, he lost it.

"I said, 'You ain't getting that goddamned flag!' "

The funeral director calmed him down, but few of the families knew that Bahr, too, had been in combat. He'd seen young men die in World War II and would see more in Korea. Bringing them home for burial etched emotions deep into his soul.

"You don't really understand combat 'til you've been in combat," he said. "It was a prerequisite (for being a military escort)."

He once had to stop a grieving mother from jumping into the grave with her son after they lowered the casket. Another time, he and another escort teamed to take home twin brothers who had been killed moments apart by the same enemy soldier.

"(The service) was in a town of 1,500," Bahr said. "According to the police, there were 1,600 people at the funeral."

The Army did nothing at the time to counsel Bahr and the others on the emotional trauma they brought home with them from the war, let alone preparing them to deal with the families as military escorts.

"There were times when you'd just want to go someplace and cry," he said. "At times I thought, 'How inadequate am I to try to do this?' There was no psychologist -- nobody to give you insight. So you drank. I'm not proud of that."

Married and a father, one day at home he accompanied the family to church. He knew he had to preempt his self-destruction.

"I realized I had to stop (drinking)," Bahr said. So he did.

His military escort duty left him with mixed emotions.

"I have some wonderful memories and met some wonderful people," he said.

Conversely, when his duty ended, he was a buck sergeant with a family and needed a promotion to upgrade his pay. He could do that by signing on for a tour in Korea beginning in July 1950, as did most of the other 300 military escorts at Fort Sheridan. Once there, though, he said he shut down emotionally. He performed his duties in reconnaissance, but got close to no one. He knew a buddy today could be in a casket tomorrow, to be taken home someday by a uniformed military escort wearing white gloves and a black arm band.

"I didn't make friends," he said. "I didn't talk to anybody. I'd go from one day to the next, and it was a good day if you made it 'til the next."

Captured by the North Koreans and Chinese, he escaped and found his way back to his unit about a month later.

While in Korea, he ran into a soldier he had known from Fort Sheridan who was among the many military escorts invited to Bahr's wedding in 1948. They were the only two escorts still alive from that day. All the others had died in Korea.

"And of the 300 men who were military escorts, maybe 50 survived the Korean War," Bahr said.

Which is why, now, Bahr won't attend Memorial Day services at the national cemetery in Santa Nella or anywhere else. He's endured too much death and brought too many young men home for their final salute. To this day, he remembers the sadness of each service as if it happened yesterday, handing yet another folded Old Glory to yet another grieving mother.

" 'This is your flag presented to you by order of the president of the United States and a grateful nation in memory of the supreme sacrifice of your son,' " he still can recite without pause.

"You took your hat off. You touched the casket. You gave the final salute. Then you backed away."

Bahr lives in Stockton.

Gentle letters tell family of deaths in two wars

May 28, 2006

Johnnie Santini never got to meet her Uncle Clarence. He was killed in World War I, six years before she was born.

Nor did the 80-year-old Escalon woman get to bid her brother, Ed Williamson, a proper goodbye. One of her five relatives who survived the attack on Pearl Harbor, Ed died later during World War II when Japanese kamikazes sank the carrier USS Bismarck Sea near Iwo Jima in 1945.

Because some people at the front took the time to write detailed letters to members of her family, Memorial Days bear an incredible amount of meaning for Santini. It's the same for other families who received similar letters from the front, now often kept in albums or collections and handed down from generation to generation.

Joan Barnett Lee / The Modesto Bee
Johnnie Santini with family album containing remembrances of her relatives who died in both World Wars.

Santini knows how her uncle and her brother died, and can pass their stories on to her children and grandchildren.

"I'm glad I've been able to get as much stuff as I could," Santini said.

These letters were written with a particular eloquence, bearing a poetic form of writing we seldom see in today's instant, edited world of e-mails and text messaging. They reflect the mood of their time as the authors tried to help families cope with their losses, and nothing was more personal than a handwritten letter from someone who was there.

A woman named Maude Cleveland, a Red Cross representative in France, used a fountain pen to write a three-page letter after Santini's uncle, Clarence Williamson, died north of Paris in May 1918.

"Dear Mother:

I have just come back from your boy's funeral. The enclosed cedar is from a tree near his grave in the beautiful French cemetery here in Beauvais. The enclosed flowers are from his coffin."

Clarence Williamson, a Louisiana native, had been shot in the left leg, Cleveland explained. It shattered his thigh bone, infection set in and he died an hour after surgeons tried to remove the leg.

"The boy went quietly and easily to sleep under the anesthetic. He lived for an hour after the operation, but never regained consciousness. Captain Jackson and Lieut. Lowrie of the American Red Cross and Dr. Lewis, Chaplain of the American Red Cross, were with him when he breathed his last. He did not suffer."

Her words describing the funeral were simply stirring.

"As the coffin covered with the French and American flag passed, everyone stopped in the streets to salute the American soldier as he went by."

His honor guard, she said, included veterans of the 1870-71 Franco-Prussian War.

"At the close of the burial service, they dipped their flag in salute to touch your son's flag-covered coffin."

She closed with words that ring as true today to the families of those killed in Iraq as they did to the families of those who died in the brutal conflict.

"No American is buried with his brother -- Americans in the cemetery here without a special prayer for his family at home -- for we know that the bravery of American mothers is as great as that of their sons."

The Williamson family would get another such letter a month shy of 27 years later. Johnnie Santini's brother, Ed, was aboard the battleship California when the Japanese bombed Pearl Harbor on Dec. 7, 1941. He initially was listed as missing in action, but turned up alive.

"He'd been picked up by the USS Astoria, a cruiser," Santini said. "One of the fellows there said, 'My God, you should be dead.' "

Ed Williamson later was assigned to the USS Bismarck Sea. On Feb. 21, 1945, Japanese kamikaze planes targeted the carrier near Iwo Jima in the final days of the war in the Pacific's most famous battle. Two of them crashed into the ship a minute or so apart, turning the ship into an inferno.

Capt. J.L. Pratt gave the "abandon ship" order, and Ed "Willy" Williamson and the hundreds of other sailors jumped into the water. He was among the 318 who died. Two weeks later, Williamson's wife received a letter from Pratt, and eventually gave it to Santini.

"Willy was known to have left the ship but did not reappear on any of the rescue vessels, nor was he found by other vessels in the area and I am afraid that he lost his life in the water, Pratt wrote. I read the Navy memorial service for him the following morning from the destroyer which rescued me.

Willy was one of the favorites of the ship and was well thought of by all his shipmates. ... May you get some solace from his memory and knowledge that he gave his life in the service of his country. We will fight all the harder because of him, to bring this war to a close."

Perhaps now more than ever, Santini appreciates these letters. One links her to the uncle she never got to know.

"I only heard my father talk about him," she said.

The other rekindles images of the strapping, handsome brother she lost. Memories that give Memorial Day its true meaning.

Johnnie Santini died in 2013.

Nightmares recall at-sea terror from 1944

October 3, 2006

In the middle of the night, with no warning, the images can return.

They leave Walt Laukkanen sweating, trembling and send his arms flailing before he is jolted into consciousness.

"I still have the nightmares," the 83-year-old Modestan said.

Images, he said, of the mind-numbing moment when he likely saved two ships and their crews because he followed his instincts and reacted so quickly. Yet it's a story he mostly kept to himself until just a couple of months ago. One midnight in late summer 1944, Laukkanen worked watch duty aboard the SS Anchorage Victory, a merchant marine cargo ship.

A junior-grade lieutenant in the Navy, Laukkanen was assigned to the ship that carried goods, arms and explosives to the battle zones. The Victory series followed the more well-known Liberty ships, and both played significant roles in keeping American troops supplied during World War II.

Debbie Noda / The Modesto Bee
Walt Laukkanen tells of a terrifying night at sea while wife Milda listens.

This particular moonless night, the Anchorage Victory steamed through enemy infested waters in blackout conditions. No radio, sonar or running lights and no destroyer escort. The ship was heading home to San Francisco after dropping off ordnance for the invasion of the Philippines.

"It took you about 10 minutes to get acclimated with your eyes (to the darkness)," Laukkanen said. "But I knew something was out there."

A Japanese submarine or destroyer?

"I had no idea," he said. "I just sensed something."

In a flash, he noticed water foaming off the hull of a much larger ship on a collision course with the Anchorage Victory. From his position a deck below the bridge, he sounded general quarters, turned on the running lights and hit the whistle twice, ordering a hard port turn.

Running at 10 knots, the Anchorage Victory rolled as it veered to the left, tossing anything that wasn't secured to the deck, Laukkanen said. Only about 20 feet separated the ships. They were that close to disaster at sea, he said.

"You could see the (blades of the propellers) from both ships out of the water," Laukkanen said. "They were like eggbeaters."

As the ships passed and the danger subsided, crew members from each yelled out their call numbers. Only then did Laukkanen recognize the other ship as a Navy troop transport capable of carrying nearly 2,000 soldiers plus landing craft.

"It would have been a catastrophe," Laukkanen said.

When his duty ended, he felt the magnitude of what he had done.

"He went back to his bunk and shook all night long," said Milda Laukkanen, Walt's wife, who worked as a draftswoman at the Mare Island shipbuilding yard in Vallejo during the war.

Yet for this, he received little more than a "good job, Laukkanen" from the ship's captain.

"You weren't allowed to talk about anything that happened," he said. "That's how it was. A few people patted me on the back. Other than that, it was all quiet on the western front."

What captain, asleep while his ship nearly collided with a troop transport, would make a show of honoring Laukkanen? To do so would be to draw attention to the incident, and anything bad or near bad always reflects poorly on the captain.

Laukkanen returned to civilian life after the war, teaching briefly in Berkeley before moving to the valley and spending 32 years as a metal shop instructor at Downey High and Modesto Junior College.

Walt retired in 1983 and worked their almond ranch near Waterford.

Milda became a noted artist who painted a number of watercolors displayed at the Casa de Modesto retirement home, where the Laukkanens now live.

Walt tried to bury that horrific moment, but his memory won't let him. He spoke of it only sparingly, Milda said.

"I got a little bit out of him," she said. "He was having nightmares, but he didn't give any details. He didn't even tell his parents what had happened. His father would have been so proud."

In fact, Walt didn't open up in any kind of detail until August. Dave Woods, who taught with Laukkanen at Downey, got him to tell more of his story.

"This incident is even more significant to me because my own father, who was a veteran of World War II, could have been on that very Navy transport that Laukkanen diverted from catastrophe," Woods said.

It's a moment Laukkanen has relived many, many times since. The unforgettable thought of what might have happened and how many people might have died had he simply ignored his instincts.

Ships' close call sounds familiar to Ceres man

October 10, 2006

From the voice mail and the e-mail:

TWO SHIPS IN THE NIGHT - Last week, I wrote about Walt Laukkanen of Modesto, who was a junior-grade lieutenant in the Navy, assigned to a Merchant Marine ship during World War II.

He described how he likely saved the SS Anchorage Victory by spotting a Navy troop transport ship headed right for it on a jet-black night in October 1944. He sounded general quarters and gave the horn two blasts demanding a hard port turn. The ships avoided colliding only by just feet. Laukkanen, 83, said he still has nightmares about the incident.

Thursday, I received a phone call from Carl Reinhardt of Ceres, who had read the column.

"I was on that other ship," Reinhardt said.

He not only remembers the incident; he wrote about it after the war. And Wednesday, he took his descriptions to the Casa de Modesto retirement community where Laukkanen now lives and met the man who prevented a tragedy at sea.

Reinhart, 84, was a member of the Army Signal Corps headed to New Guinea in the fall of 1944. When he read the column about Laukkanen, he instantly remembered the incident, which happened somewhere west of the Philippines.

The Navy transport, carrying 2,000, was supposed to go directly to New Guinea in late summer of 1944, Reinhart said. Because hundreds of U.S. warships were leaving New Guinea for the invasion of the Philippines' island of Leyte, Reinhart's ship spent nearly two months staying out of their way. It was during that time the near-collision happened.

"When we were in the warmer-weather areas, a number of us would sleep out on deck because the lower decks (bunk areas) got foul," Reinhart said.

So he was outside when the ship changed course suddenly, even though he doesn't remember waking because of any sudden movements. But the soldiers did talk about it the next day.

In a 16-page memoir, Reinhart explained that the Navy troop ship -- he never wrote down the ship's name, because he was an Army guy -- traveled without escort through enemy-controlled waters.

He titled the document "My Life in the Service, Nov. '42 to Jan. '46." His entry about the close call is on Page 9.

"The only encounter of any kind happened about three weeks into our journey," Reinhart wrote. "We came upon another ship at night that didn't give us the correct identification signal. Immediately, our ship reversed direction and left the area at full speed."

That was pretty much it. OK, so his description wasn't movie-script dramatic. But it matched the time frame and incident Laukkanen described. After the war, Reinhart returned to farming in Ceres. Laukkanen taught for 32 years at Downey High and Modesto Junior College.

Even though they lived in the same county for more than five decades, they probably never were closer in physical proximity than they were that night in the Pacific -- until Wednesday. That's when Reinhart called Laukkanen and set up a meeting. It was a reunion of sorts involving two men who once were 20 feet apart in the Pacific.

"To have that (incident) bothering him this long, and to find someone who recognized what had happened -- he was really excited," Reinhart said. "He said, 'This puts the dots together now.' "

"Walter's eyes closed when he met him," said Milda Laukkanen, Walt's wife. "They spent quite a bit of time talking. It's a positive thing."

The kind of thing, maybe, that will put his nightmares to rest?

"I think it will," she said.

Walt Laukkanen died in 2007 and Milda Laukkanen in 2012. Carl Reinhart lives in Ceres.

Long-abused POW wins freedom from hate

July 4, 2013

We talk -- often very loudly, proudly and sometimes defiantly -- about our freedoms.

Speech and religion, gun ownership, marriage equity, abortion, you name it.

Freedom from government intrusion into our personal lives (even as we gladly hand over personal information to the social networks, credit card companies and others who profit from it while hackers try to steal it).

Joan Barnett Lee / The Modesto Bee
World War II POW Leroy Myers at his Modesto home in 2013.

Indeed, freedom is an American's most valued and cherished possession.

Leroy Myers understands freedom, but in a much different and perhaps deeper way than many folks.

The 93-year-old Modestan, alongside his father, spent all but a few days of his time in World War II as a prisoner of war, most of it in Japan. The Japanese took away his possessions, including his clothing. They beat him with sticks. They kicked and punched him. They starved him down to 80 pounds on a diet of vermin-riddled food. They forced him to carry sacks of concrete that outweighed him by 20 pounds.

They forced Myers and other POWs to dig their own mass grave, telling them they would be executed the moment Allied forces invaded Japan.

"It couldn't have been any worse, or you'd be dead," he said.

Instead, atomic bombs fell on Hiroshima and Nagasaki in August 1945, bringing an abrupt end to the war. Japan surrendered, and the soldiers who were supposed to kill Myers and the others fled the camp to save their hides. Suddenly, Myers was free again. Free to go home, to come and go as he pleased, to work -- for pay -- wherever he chose. To voice his opinions without fear of flogging or death.

And perhaps most poignant, he was free to forgive.

"I don't hate the Japanese," he says today. "Oh, sure, I hated them when I got back. Of course, you hate the people who beat you and loved doing it. It's hard to forgive them."

But, he said, it is impossible for him to hate the Japanese woman who approached Myers and his equally emaciated father, Charles, as they worked along a road near the prison camp. She dropped two cooked sweet potatoes near them as she walked by, knowing she could have been executed for doing so.

Courtesy of The Modesto Bee
Leroy Myers in 2012 at the dam he was forced to build as a POW in Japan.

"We stuffed them in our shirts and ate them later," Myers said. "I never tasted a candy bar that tasted better."

Nor could he hate one particular honcho -- a civilian overseer in the prison camp -- who once hid him beneath a blanket, knowing that if Japanese soldiers saw the pneumonia- stricken American in such bad shape, they would have killed him.

No, there's only so much time in life, and he doesn't want to waste it on hate.

His time as a POW mirrors that of Louis Zamperini, the Olympic athlete whose experiences were described in the book "Unbroken."
Myers' father, Charles Leroy Myers Sr., went in early 1941 to Wake Island in the South Pacific as a heavy-equipment operator. He worked for a contractor hired by the government to fortify the Marine base on the island, and needed more operators. So Leroy Myers joined his dad in February to run cranes, drag lines and other machinery for what then was a whopping

$230 per month.

Within hours of bombing Pearl Harbor on Dec. 7, the Japanese also hit Wake. The Marines and other military, along with 1,200 private contract workers on the island, repelled the first wave and inflicted damage on the Japanese planes. Leroy, 21 at the time, later learned he'd been inducted by the Navy as a seaman first class.

The battle lasted 15 days, until the Japanese finally seized the island Dec. 23, taking 1,606 prisoners, including more than 1,100 civilian contractors, according to various history websites.

The Japanese kept 98 U.S. civilian workers on the island and sent the others north to Japan and China, but not before making some of the prisoners -- Leroy Myers among them -- witness the beheading of one American who had escaped and been recaptured.

Leroy said he and his father were allowed to stay together because the Japanese culture values family. Even so, they spent the rest of the war waiting to be killed, just as the Japanese executed the 98 who remained on Wake Island.

Myers and his father steamed to Japan in the cargo hold of a ship, given only a cup of water and a fistful of rice each day.

They arrived in Sasebo and were taken to a labor camp in the hills several miles away, where they built the Soto Dam at a horrific cost. Fifty-three Americans and many Japanese died during construction. Father and son survived because they relied on each other. When the elder Myers injured his back, Leroy carried twice as many 100-pound concrete sacks each day to make up the difference.

When the POWs had to fight off stomach worms they got from the disgusting food they received, the elder Myers had the answer.

"They didn't let us bring anything (from Wake)," Leroy said. "But they didn't know anything about chewing tobacco. My dad had a carton of Day's Work, and they laughed at him and let him bring it. He remembered that when he was a kid, they'd take a piece of chewing tobacco and wrap it in a piece of meat and use it to worm the dogs."

Hence, they swallowed a small piece of the stuff once a week.

"We never had a problem with the worms," Leroy said.

But there was never enough food to match the calories they burned lugging heavy sacks of concrete across the gorge to the dam's mixing room. Never enough to replace the energy they spent digging graves when one of their own died. Dysentery made the food pass right through them.
The mixing room itself filled with a thick, choking dust when they emptied the sacks.

They endured the cold Japanese winters in skimpy clothing that hung on their thin frames.

 Leroy once contemplated suicide and actually climbed a railroad trestle to commit the deed. But he knew if he died, his dad wouldn't survive. They were sent to another camp at Fukuoka and were there when the war ended. They'd lost far more than four years of their lives to imprisonment. After they were captured, the Navy told the contracting firm it would no longer pay for their services. The money stopped going home to Chico, and the family home fell to foreclosure.

And because the Japanese refused to allow them to write letters home, Sylvia Myers died in 1944 never knowing her husband and son still were alive, nor did they know until they returned to the States after the war that she had died.

They had to sue the U.S. government to get their rightful 44 months of back pay, and Leroy used his to buy a ranch near Chico. Charles Myers never fully recovered from the physical ailments and died in the 1950s. Leroy Myers, meanwhile, went on to work for Del Monte, which brought him to Modesto.

He returned twice to visit Wake Island -- once shortly after the war and again in the 1990s. And he went back to Japan over the past Memorial Day -- yes, to Sasebo and the dam he helped build -- to attend a ceremony at the elaborate monument remembering the 53 Americans and 14 Japanese who died there. He paid his own way, and Stars and Stripes chronicled the event.

Myers said the current residents of Sasebo claim to be completely unaware of the horrors that went on at the camp. "They don't want to talk about it. They don't want to admit they bombed Honolulu and started the war."

But he can't hate them for it. He told me he dreamed one night of a giant book that rose out of the ocean. One page held a message he since has forgotten. The facing page bore these words: "Hate is destroying the world."

"I think about the little woman and the sweet potatoes," he said. "And I think about the honcho who hid me when I was dying. I'm 93 years old. I've lived a good life. I'm going to die one of these days. I am not going to waste the time I have left on Earth hating."

He is free indeed.

Leroy Myers lives in Modesto and, at 97, continues to write poetry.

Survivor finds life a wonder

February 16, 2014

Peter Harringer will celebrate his 80th birthday next month.

He's in good shape mentally and physically, a man who retired after a long career at the old Contadina food processing plant in Riverbank and now owns a photography business.

That he's completing his eighth decade isn't unusual. Instead, Harringer wonders how he ever lived to nearly 80 in the first place. How, from the time he was 8 years old, did he survive 27 months in a Nazi concentration camp during World War II? Why, in a camp that housed more than 15,000 children throughout the war, was he among the 96 who weren't sent by rail to the death camps of Treblinka or Auschwitz?

The Modesto Bee
Peter Harringer holds photo of himself as child.

"I have no idea," he said. "I don't know."

Imagine being a young boy trying to navigate that part of life in a time and place when the world was, indeed, coming apart at the seams. Imagine being bounced from family to family in the ghettos, at their mercy and never a priority. Imagine being always the outsider, until living inside prison walls became a way of life, and all before your ninth birthday. Harringer's story blends tragedy, will and a bit of luck.

He was born in Breslau, Germany (now part of Poland), in 1934 to a Protestant woman and Hungarian Jew who worked as a window dresser in Budapest. "They didn't marry," he said, which is why his surname is the same as his mother's and not his father's, which he said he doesn't know. He remembers being in school, where every student saluted Adolf Hitler each morning.

"I saw him once on his birthday," he said. "There was a birthday parade for him in Breslau."

When World War II broke out, Harringer's mother told the Germans about his father, which put 5-year-old Peter in the Nazis' radar as well.

"My dad, I think he died in Auschwitz," Harringer said. "I was a 'mischling' (German for mixture)."

His mother handed him off to others to raise, and he didn't see her again until 1941, when they met briefly in Berlin.

"I was 6 years old," he said. "She brought me some honey-flavored candies."

He became reliant upon others for food, clothing and security, and lived for a time in a nunnery, where he converted to Catholicism.

Courtesy of The Modesto Bee
Peter Harringer's U.S. Citizenship document, which he received in 1965.

"I've never been in a synagogue and I never went to a Protestant church," he said.

A nun named Sister Caritas looked after him and hid him from the Nazis. "She knew my mother had turned my father's name in," he said.

He also stayed briefly with a woman named Schmidt who treated him horribly.

"She'd force-feed me with a wooden spoon, shoving potatoes down my throat," Harringer said. "Sometimes she made me take baths with her."

When he learned later that bombs struck the woman's home and killed her, he felt no sadness.

He lived briefly with a Jewish family that had a 13-year-old daughter. One day he returned from confession, and she asked him, "How do you feel?"

"As clean as an angel," Harringer said he replied. "She told her father what I'd said, and I got a whipping for comparing myself to an angel."

One day he awoke to an eerie quiet in the home.

"Everybody was gone. They were trying to escape Germany," he said. The church tried to hide him. So did a nurse named Frida.

"She took me underground all over Berlin," Harringer said.

Finally, he was taken in by a Jewish family that lived in a part of Berlin still standing today, he said. He came home after playing in the snow one day, and the mom was packing all of his belongings.

"We're being fetched," she told him. "Take everything with you."

"I never saw them again," Harringer said.

A German soldier ushered him into a truck at gunpoint, and Harringer soon found himself en route to a women's prison. There, he was interviewed by Alois Brunner, aide to Adolph Eichmann, the Nazi SS officer who oversaw the mass relocation of Jews to the ghettos and death camps. Brunner himself ordered the deaths of more than 140,000 Jews during the war. As recently as 2003, still wanted for war crimes, Brunner supposedly was living in Syria (he would be 102 now).

Escorted into a dimly lit room at the prison, Harringer noticed a gun on the desk.

"As I walked in, the pistol went away and a big red apple came out," he said. Brunner talked to him for what seemed like a long time, questioning where he'd been and the families he'd lived with over the years. When Harringer listed one of the families he'd stayed with, the Collmans, Brunner told him smugly they had been captured and shot. The boy found it difficult to care much because of the way they had treated him.

"And I never got that apple," Harringer said.

The Nazis put him on a train and sent him to Terezin, a town named for the Habsburg Empress Maria Theresa in what is now the Czech Republic. The concentration camp there housed more than 150,000 Jews, 88,000 of whom were sent to Auschwitz, Treblinka or other camps to be killed, while others died from torture and malnutrition at Terezin.

Those in the camp existed on a diet of bread and margarine, and whenever people ask Harringer today what he thought about while in the camp, he tells them: "Food. I was always hungry."

Other senses trigger recollections as well.

"People don't understand what a concentration camp smells like," he said, referring to the stench of death, along with the overwhelming smell of the living. "Nobody had soap. There was no deodorant. The men stunk. The Nazis stunk. I certainly wouldn't have lived like that. And there were lots of fleas and bedbugs. Flea bites went away in a couple of days. Bedbug bites lasted a long time."

Why did the Nazis, who knew he was a mischling, spare him? "I don't know," Harringer said.

He does remember this: "The Nazis gave us Catholics a place to worship. There was a loft, with a big crucifix. I don't remember anybody preaching, but we could go up there and pray."

The collapse of the Third Reich meant the end of the war in Europe and Soviets marching into Terezin to liberate the camp. After sending him to a castle that once housed the Hitler youth, they asked Harringer, only 11 years old, where he wanted to go. He chose England, and stayed there for more than a decade through the 1948 London Olympics, the funeral of King George VI and the coronation of Queen Elizabeth II in 1952.

In 1958, he visited his mother in Europe. She never explained why she left him so vulnerable, so endangered. She never apologized.

"What happened happened," said Harringer, who came to the United States in 1960 and became a citizen five years later. "I never called her 'mother.' But as soon as I saw her, I knew it was my mom."

He returned to Terezin in 1997, visiting the camp he was forced to call home for more than two years and finding his name and inmate ID -- 10676-I/87 -- on a roster there. During the trip, he also visited Auschwitz, where so many of his Jewish friends died.

"To me, it's the saddest place," Harringer said, ever mindful that he could have been shipped there to die instead of now preparing to turn 80 in Oakdale 16 days from today.

"I still wonder why I'm still alive," he said. "I ask myself that all the time."

Harringer lives in Oakdale and, after the column appeared, frequently spoke to school groups and service clubs.

Holocaust exhibits vivid 11 years later

June 16, 2009

Whenever a major event occurs and you have even a casual connection to the people or the place, it rekindles images and memories.

Last week, a hatemonger entered the U.S. Holocaust Museum in Washington, D.C., and opened fire, killing a security guard.

The Holocaust Museum memorializes the murders of 6 million Jews and the horrific treatment of those who somehow escaped death at the hands of the Nazis during World War II. It also creates a visual display of genocide in hopes it would never happen again, though it has in eastern Europe, Asia and Africa.

The museum is a solemn place, mostly quiet except for the shuffling of feet and an occasional gasp. Three floors, all about death and desperation.

I visited the Holocaust Museum many years ago, and the memory lingers.

For two months early in 1998, I worked in McClatchy's D.C. bureau. Michael Doyle, who covers valley issues for McClatchy, had taken a year's leave of absence. I was one of several reporters who took turns filling in for him.

One afternoon, Doyle called just to say hello and to see how things were going. I mentioned I was going to the Holocaust Museum the next day. He suggested that I plan on doing something uplifting afterward, because it is an extremely emotional and heart-wrenching exhibit.

At that time -- the procedures might have since changed -- visitors buying their tickets were given a starting time to control the foot traffic through the museum.

Precisely on time, the elevator doors opened and all of us with 11 a.m. tickets filed in. It took us to the third floor to begin the tour. We worked our way, floor to floor, back down toward the lobby. Every group pretty much stayed together throughout the tour. My group included an elderly couple who spoke English through thick accents I guessed to be eastern European.

The photos and exhibits were indeed mind-numbing. The cruelty and suffering inflicted upon Holocaust victims was unfathomable. Photos of the death camps, the mass graves and emaciated Jews were as disturbing as anything I'd ever seen.

Other exhibits were more subtle, yet just as moving. One consisted of a large collection of shoes taken from the victims before they went to the showers and, ultimately, their deaths.

On the second floor, there were some photos showing a group of children in one of the camps. The same elderly couple behind me in line stood looking at them, and suddenly the gentleman started shaking and sobbing. As he pointed toward the photo, he began to lose his balance. His wife grabbed him by one arm. I took the other, and we eased him to a bench.

This man, the wife explained, had been one of the young boys in the photo. He began crying uncontrollably. The reporter in me wanted to hang around, hoping he'd tell me his story. How had he survived? But as the wife consoled and hugged her husband, it was clear he was in no mood to talk about it, and certainly not to me.

It was his moment to relive the pain, to hurt and to grieve for those in the photo who didn't survive or have since died. He certainly didn't need my intrusion.

I resumed the tour and finished it, moved by the experience and numbed by the moment.

And 11 years later, a man filled with the same kind of hate that led to the Holocaust reminded us why the museum is needed.

Japanese soldier's flag needs rest of its story told

February 26, 2012

Behind any piece in a museum exhibit, there is a back story that tells what it represented, who or what created it, how it was obtained. Often, that back story is every bit as interesting or thought-provoking as the item itself.

Consider a silk flag mounted inside the Commemorative Air Force Central California Valley Squadron's tiny but growing museum at the Modesto Airport. This particular piece of memorabilia came home with a Marine who fought in the Pacific campaign during World War II. It once belonged to a Japanese soldier. It bears the sun circle of Japan and is surrounded by numerous Japanese writing symbols.

The flag somehow went to another Marine who never left the states. Family lore suggests he won it in a poker game at Camp Lejeune, N.C. When he died, he bequeathed the flag to his daughter, Michael Edwards Rowe of Santa Cruz. Last month, she gave the flag to Dee Rowe, her father-in-law and a retired dentist in Modesto, out of respect for his military service.

Dee Rowe, 91, flew a B-29 bomber nicknamed Banzai during the war. When Banzai wasn't flying,

Joan Barnett Lee / The Modesto Bee
Dee Rowe, a World War II B-29 pilot, with a flag that once belonged to a Japanese soldier.

Rowe parked it near the Enola Gay of atomic bomb fame on the tarmac at Tinian Island. Rowe also is a member of the Commemorative Air Force group, whose clubhouse is the airport's 84-year-old Hangar 1.

Rowe recently put the flag on display, but not until a friend prevailed upon a Japanese-language translator and culture expert in Aptos to unravel the mystery of the jottings on the flag.

Hence, the aforementioned back story:

In Japan, the flag is called a Hinomaru yosegaki, meaning it was passed around to friends and family members who signed it for a soldier going off to join the Imperial Army. A good-luck flag, they'd call it in English. This particular flag, the translator deciphered, belonged to a soldier named Tatsumi Kato. The most interesting aspect? The writings were from his baseball teammates at the NKG company, an auto parts manufacturer founded in 1919.

The company still exists, and its president is named Taro Kato. Any relation to the soldier by the same last name and whose flag is now in a Modesto museum?

I sent an e-mail to the company to see if they were related, and with a faint hope of learning the fate of Tatsumi Kato. Faint became futile when an NKG representative replied. No such luck.

"Kato is a common family name in Japan and there is at present more than 70 employees named Kato in the company," wrote Ken Akimoto of NKG's public relations department. "So, it is almost impossible to find out someone who has any relationship with Tatsumi Kato."

Oh, well. It was worth a try. Yet the unknowns about such a museum piece simply add to the intrigue. Yes, a captured Japanese flag is interesting to war buffs. But to know even a little bit about the Japanese soldier it belonged to leaves you wondering:

Who was this person? Did he have a wife and kids back home? Did he surrender? Did he flee and leave the flag behind when the American troops stormed the island? Was he killed in action? Did he take an American life? And knowing he played America's national pastime humanizes him as well, especially when you consider American major leaguers including San Francisco's Lefty O'Doul introduced the sport to Japan in the 1930s.

In essence, NKGs company team replicated the company baseball clubs that once flourished in the United States. Just look to the sawmills in the foothills, where West Side in Tuolumne City and Pickering in Standard near Sonora were known to hire former minor-leaguers as much for their ability to handle the lumber in the batter's boxes as cutting it inside the mills.

"When we mention (to visitors) that it's from a baseball team, people say, 'Baseball? Prior to the war?' " said Ron Thomas, the museum's curator. "Baseball was sought after in Japan just like it was here."

Which is the point of a history museum -- to teach visitors something they didn't know about the past.

And as the scribblings on the Japanese good-luck flag prove, knowing at least some of the story behind the artifact makes it even more intriguing.

Dee Rowe died in 2014.

Valley shared in WWII Wronging of Japanese Americans

April 19, 2015

While in Washington, D.C., many years ago, I spent an incredible Saturday afternoon in the Smithsonian's American history museum.

Nothing made a greater lasting impression than the exhibit of the internment camps where more than 120,000 Japanese Americans were imprisoned during World War II following Japan's attack on Pearl Harbor in 1941.

In fact, the very first photo on the wall entering the exhibit hit home because it depicted a family living in a horse stall. It was taken at the fairgrounds in Stockton, which were used as an assembly center where the internees were processed before going to their respective camps.

This week, a New Jersey auctioneer – under fire from the Japanese American Citizens League and others – aborted plans to sell hundreds of artifacts that came from the internment camps. The controversy resonated here in the Valley, as well.

Why? Because thousands of Japanese Americans who lived here were forced to go to the camps. Many farmed in Turlock, Livingston, Delhi, Atwater, Merced and Stockton. Anti-Japanese sentiment existed well before Pearl Harbor, though.

The state of California established a farming community in Delhi in 1919 specifically to "prevent Japanese farmers from purchasing the 8,000-acre tract," according to Sarah Lim of the Merced County Historical Society. And when a group of Japanese settlers marched into downtown Turlock around that time, lifelong Livingston resident Sherman Kishi said, "(white residents) chased them out."

Shortly after the attack that drew America into the war, President Franklin D. Roosevelt signed an executive order commanding all of

Japanese ancestry to be relocated to the camps. It didn't matter whether they were naturalized citizens or born here, or whether they pledged their allegiance to this nation. They were forced to leave their homes and farms to report to assembly centers throughout the region, among them the fairgrounds in Merced and Turlock. Two buildings on the Stanislaus County Fairgrounds in Turlock that were used to process the Japanese Americans beginning in 1942 are still in use today. A small monument at the fairgrounds serves as a reminder.

"When we did the dedication in 2011, there were at least 80 or 90 issei (first-generation Japanese-Americans) and nisei (second-generation) who attended," Stanislaus County Fair CEO Chris Borovansky said. "There was no bitterness, no anger. They were very dignified."

They flocked to the photos posted on the walls, looking for themselves, family members or friends, he said.

"They had their own culture, their own activities, their own baseball teams," Borovansky said. "Some of them pointed to the horse stalls and said that's where they stayed."

From there, the Japanese Americans were sent to internment camps in remote and windswept hellholes like Tule Lake and Manzanar in California. Livingston's Kishi and his family were processed at the Merced fairground and sent to the Amache relocation camp in Colorado.

Bart Ah You / The Modesto Bee
Sherman Kishi was among Japanese-American citizens sent to internment camps during World War II.

"That was an event that never should have happened," Kishi said. "We were citizens. In fact, 80,000 (who were relocated). It was a wrong."

When the war ended and they were allowed to return home, many found they had to start over because they'd sold their homes and farms for a fraction of their value to opportunists, fearing they might otherwise lose them and get nothing at all.

Yet they came back to rebuild their way of life while maintaining their traditions, as well as their commitment to family, farming and their communities.

A monument dedicated in 2010 at the Merced County Fairgrounds etched in stone the names of all who came through that assembly center.

While imprisoned, most will tell you they tried to make the best of a bad situation, including creating the same kinds of arts and crafts that were supposed to go up for auction on Friday until the protests halted the sale.

"I still have what I made, and I would never sell it to anybody," Kishi said. "I made several little bird lapel pins to give my girlfriend. She's the one I married."

Which is why the New Jersey auction plan disturbed so many people regardless of ancestry. The owner of the collection simply planned to profit from the injustice done to Japanese Americans by selling to the highest bidder the artwork and crafts they made while in the camps.

The collection belongs in a museum like the Smithsonian – not in somebody's den or man cave or for-profit museum.

It needs to be where it can remind or educate visitors about one of the most unjust times in the nation's history.

Sherman Kishi lives in Livingston and talks to school students about the internment camps.

Reason for vet's survival a town away

August 9, 2009

Lonie Black and Vern Korock have lived just 17 miles apart since Black moved to Turlock in 1962.

They're both 83 years old. They've never met and, until recently, had never heard of each other.

Bart Ah You /The Modesto Bee
Lonie Black of Turlock was destined to be in the invasion of Japan.

Yet, Black survived World War II in no small part because of Korock, a longtime Modesto resident.

Every event of every kind has its intangibles, elements that affect the outcome even though the principals might need years or even a lifetime to make sense of it all.

This is one of those cases.

As a member of the Navy Seabees, Korock helped build the runway on Tinian Island in the Pacific's Northern Mariana Islands. On Aug. 6, 1945, the B-29 Enola Gay took off from Tinian to drop the first atomic bomb on Hiroshima, Japan. Three days later and 64 years ago today, another B-29, this one called Bockscar, took off from the same airfield and dropped the second bomb, this time on Nagasaki.

About 200,000 Japanese died in those two cities. The death and devastation compelled Emperor Hirohito to announce Japan's surrender to its people Aug. 15, 1945. Had they resisted, the Americans planned to launch Operation Downfall, the code name for the invasion of Japan. That is where Black would have been.

U.S. military officials knew such an invasion would be a bloodbath. They expected 1,000 American deaths an hour during the early going, a minimum of 125,000 overall and possibly 1 million casualties (dead and wounded) to end the war. Countless more Japanese soldiers and citizens would have died as well.

"They said it would have made D-Day seem like a piece of cake," Black said.

By the time he turned 19, Black had fought and survived three major campaigns: New Guinea and the re-takings of Leyte and Luzon in the Philippines. But invading Japan would be different, he knew. If Operation Downfall had gotten the go-ahead, he and the other engineers of the 11th Airborne Division would have been

Courtesy of Lonie Black
Lonie Black during World War II.

among the first troops to hit the shores, even before the infantry. And, likely, among the first of the casualties.

Instead, the bombs compelled the Japanese to surrender. Instead of dying in a flaming troop transport that took a direct kamikaze hit, or from machine-gun fire on a beach, Black walked through the door of his parents' home in Southern California on Christmas Eve 1945.

"Mom didn't know I was coming," he said.

For that he thanks men like Korock.

The Navy turned him away when he tried to enlist in 1942 because he was color blind. A year later, he found a way into the war.

"I heard about the Seabees," Korock said. "I went in; they took me in Portland, Ore."

They sent him to Norfolk, Va., for boot camp, and then to Gulfport, Miss., for advanced training. He soon shipped out to the Enewetak Atoll in the Marshall Islands, where his outfit built an airstrip, using as its base coral they dragged in from ocean.

"The prettiest airplane landing I ever saw in my life was a Corsair on that airstrip," Korock said. "The whole island was only about a quarter-mile wide."

Vernon Korock helped build the airstrip on Tinian Island that launched the Enola Gay

In late July 1944, American forces began their invasion of Tinian. Even before the Marines drove off the Japanese, Korock and the Seabees were on the island and building the runway that would play such a vital role. Within a year, they had built the world's largest airfield, complete with four 8,500-foot runways and home to 1,000 B-29 bombers, among them the Enola Gay and the Bockscar.

On July 26, 1945, Black's 19th birthday, the heavy cruiser USS Indianapolis dropped anchor off Tinian's coast. It carried the innards of the "Little Boy," the first of the atomic bombs. The components were brought on the island in a shroud of secrecy.

"We had no idea there was any atomic bomb on the island," Korock said. "There was one part of the island, where the A-bomb was, that was secured from everybody but the upper echelon."

Four days later, two Japanese torpedoes sank the Indianapolis.

The departure of the Enola Gay on Aug. 6 was no different from other bombing runs to most of those stationed on Tinian. They didn't know until after the Bockscar dropped the second A-bomb, "Fat Man," a few days later what had happened.

"Today, everybody would have known because they let the news out," Korock said. "Back then, they never let the news out."

Emperor Hirohito's surrender announcement told the world the war finally would end. No one felt a greater sense of relief than Black.

"Knowing what our future was going to be like (if the Americans had invaded), I cried like a baby, and I'm not ashamed to admit it," he said.

The 11th Airborne were among the first Americans on the ground in

Japan, and Black was understandably mistrustful of the Japanese. But they encountered no resistance.

After returning to the states, he worked in his father's orchard and then went to work for Frito-Lay, which is what brought Black, his wife, Virginia, and their family to the valley in 1962.

Korock met his wife, Leona, at the Merry Gardens skating rink in Modesto before he went off to war. Upon his return, they started their family.

Dropping the atomic bombs remains as controversial today as it was after Hiroshima and Nagasaki, with Iran and North Korea emerging as rogue nations with nuclear arms programs. The difference between then and now? The United States used the bombs to end a war.

The vast majority of World War II veterans believe the United States did what it had to do by dropping the bombs.

"I wear an Airborne hat all the time when we go out to eat or whatever," Black said. "I'll have people come up and say, 'You were in World War II?' "

Occasionally, someone will remark, " 'You shouldn't have dropped the A-bomb on those poor people,' " Black said. "And I'll say, 'Would you rather have had 200,000 of their people die or have us invade the islands and lose half of our army?' "

Korock believes President Truman's decision to use the bombs saved more lives than they took.

"I don't think he had any choice," Korock said. "He couldn't gamble on losing another 100,000 or so against losing a few. Look at all the lives we lost taking some of those islands."

Black, dead certain he would have died in an invasion, is ever so thankful to those whose hard work and determination prevented it. That includes Korock, the next-town-over neighbor he's never met.

"The way I look at it," Black said, "I've been living on borrowed time for 64 years."

Lonie Black died in 2013. Vernon Korock died in 2017.

Figure 1Darryl Bush / The Modesto Bee
Doris Wanty, left, and Adeline Ellison with their Congressional Gold Medals.

Honor due WWII women fliers coming

August 25, 2009

Army brass initially fought to keep them from flying for their country. And when they were through, they had to wait more than three decades to be considered military "veterans."

The role of women pilots during World War II was highly underplayed and clearly underappreciated.

Now, with President Barack Obama having signed a bill into law last month, members of the Women Airforce Service Pilots finally will get some recognition. Sometime later this year or early next, many of the nearly 300 surviving WASPs -- Adeline Ellison of Modesto and Doris Wanty of

Oakdale among them -- will go to Washington, D.C., to receive the Congressional Gold Medal, the nation's highest civilian honor.

It took a long and concerted campaign of calling members of Congress to get them to support the bill, said Ellison, who will turn 90 Sept. 26. Wanty is 86.

"They finally decided to do it," Ellison said. "There were only 300 of us left when the president signed it. We've lost three or four since. We're all getting up there (in age)."

The recognition is long overdue for the 1,074 women pilots who, working as civilians, flew military planes at home to free male pilots for combat duty. They flew everything from training planes to C-47 transports to B-17, B-24 and B-25 bombers. They flew them from the manufacturers to points of departure to the war zones. They flew them from base to base, all over the country.

All of them were civilian pilots before training to become WASPs, and "we learned to fly the Army way," Ellison said.

As a young woman in Illinois, she began flying at the urging of her father – "a just-for-fun pilot" -- she said.

"He talked me into going out and getting some flying lessons," Ellison said.

Despite the objections of Gen. Henry "Hap" Arnold, commander of the Army Air Forces, the military began using the civilian women pilots to fly its planes in 1941. Ellison, 21 at the time, jumped at the chance.

"We saw an ad in the paper from Jackie Cochran (who organized the WASP effort) wanting women pilots," Ellison said.

More than 25,000 applied, and about 1,900 were selected for the program. Of those, 1,074 earned their wings, according to author Amy Nathan in her 2001 book "Yankee Doodle Gals."

"I ferried aircraft from California to all over the U.S.," said Ellison, who was stationed at Long Beach.

Wanty spent most of her 11 months as a WASP in Texas, flying PT-17 Stearman and Vultee BT-13 Valiant training planes.

The last time she flew solo?

"In December 1944," Wanty said, referring to when the program ended.

Because they were considered civilians, they enjoyed none of the respect nor the honors those in the military received for their efforts. If a WASP died in the line of duty -- and 38 of them did -- her family had to pay to bring her body home for burial, and they were not allowed to drape an American flag over the casket, Ellison said.

"A lot of the girls would donate money to help pay," said Ellison's daughter, Andrea Holmquist.

Ellison experienced additional disappointment. When the program disbanded, she joined the newly formed Air Force reserves. By 1952, she had risen to the rank of first lieutenant. She also got married and had two children, all of which was on her military record. But while taking an Air Force class in personnel management -- the only woman in a class of 35 students -- her colonel overheard her talking about her children during a break.

"He said, 'You have children?' " Ellison said. "I said, 'Yes.' He said, 'Unless you have someone adopt your children, you can't be in the Air Force reserves.' "

He allowed her to finish the class, then had her honorably discharged. "It broke my heart," she said. She lost her retirement pay, too, she said.

A Congressional Gold Medal won't right that wrong. But it is one more step toward formally recognizing the overall lack of respect given to women -- civilians as well as those in the military -- for their roles during wartime.

When the WASPs head to Washington to pick up their medals, Wanty and Ellison plan to be there.

"We're hoping to be able to go," said Mike Wanty, Doris' husband. They have attended numerous WASP meetings over the years. But he warns, the government shouldn't wait too long to schedule the ceremony -- not with so many of the surviving WASPs and their spouses approaching 90.

"None of us are spring chickens anymore," he said.

Adeline Ellison died in June 2017. Wanty lives in Oakdale.

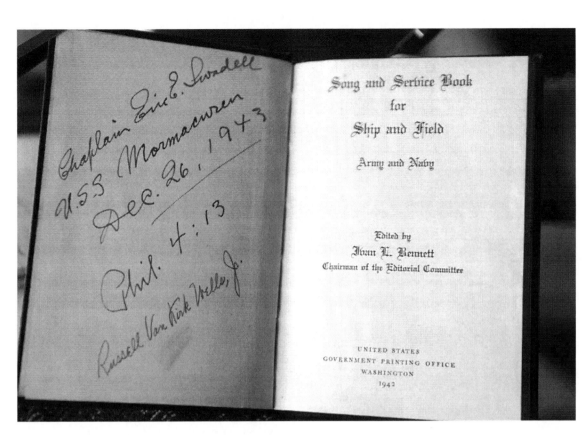

The kindness of a stranger in France returned the prayer service book of a military chaplain to his daughter in Modesto. Courtesy of The Modesto Bee.

Link to dad sent from France

April 24, 2011

For all of the Internet's pitfalls -- invasion of privacy, hackers, ID theft, computer-wrecking viruses and whatnot -- it also has some incredible benefits.

Just ask Mary Rose Shelton of Modesto. How else could a complete and total stranger halfway across the world track her down to give her a family heirloom?

This story began a couple of weeks ago when her son, Mark Shelton of San Luis Obispo, received an e-mail from a gentleman in France. The sender, Olivier Calvez, wrote that he possessed a Bible he believed originally belonged to Eric Swadell, Mary Rose's father, whose 20-year run as a military chaplain included service in World War II.

Calvez bought the book on eBay in 2006. It bore Swadell's signature, dated Dec. 26, 1943, and included the name of the ship he was on at the time, the SS Mormacwren.

The Frenchman began searching for Swadell on the Internet and found a biography. Next, in modbee.com's Legacy feature, he came across a tribute to George Shelton, Mary Rose's husband, who died in January.

Joan Barnett Lee / The Modesto Bee

Mary Rose Shelton

Calvez then went on Facebook in hopes of locating the family members named in the tribute. That's how he connected with Mark Shelton, who is an associate dean at Cal Poly San Luis Obispo. Mark forwarded Calvez's e-mail to his mom. She began a correspondence that brought her a most special gift.

"I am shipping it to you today, as it is a treasure to you," Calvez wrote April 13.

The book arrived a few days later. It wasn't a Bible, though. It was her father's "Song & Service Book for Ship & Field," which is a military chaplain's handbook detailing the services he would need to officiate at for various religions. It included the Stations of the Cross for Catholics and different rites for those of the Jewish faith.

Her father's life was interesting in its own right. Born in Denmark, he signed on as a boiler stoker on a steamship in Copenhagen in 1915. The ship was torpedoed by the Germans at the outbreak of World War I. He survived. He tried to join the British Navy but was refused because he couldn't prove he wasn't German (Danish accent and all). Then, he listened as another man with a French accent told the British recruiters he was from Canada. Swadell used the same tactic.

"They took him," Shelton said.

He fought in the Battle of the Somme and suffered a bullet wound. While awaiting treatment, the aid station was attacked. It was mustard gas. Swadell had lost his gas mask in the field when he was wounded.

"They say there are no atheists in foxholes," Shelton said. "He dug a hole, buried his head and prayed. 'OK, God, if you save me, you've got my life.' "

Swadell received a King's Badge, Britain's equivalent of America's Purple Heart. He moved to the United States, enrolling at Biola College in Los Angeles in 1923. He married and started a family, later attending a Baptist college in Kentucky and becoming a naturalized U.S. citizen in 1939.

Two years later, the Japanese bombed Pearl Harbor. He tried to enlist as a military chaplain, but was refused because of his age (45).

"So he went to the California State Guard," Shelton said, referring to the predecessor of the California National Guard.

They sent him to such hot spots as Don Pedro, Hetch Hetchy and Coarsegold, places authorities feared might be deemed targets by the enemy. But soon the U.S. military beckoned and Swadell answered.

"He related to the soldiers so well," Shelton said. "He'd done everything they were doing."

Swadell served in the Pacific Theater, on the islands of Tinian and Saipan. On troop transports, he would stand at the side of the ships and wish soldiers well as they went over the edge and into the landing craft.

"He told the story of one soldier who knelt down and said, 'Pray for me, Father,' " Shelton said. "He kissed (Swadell's ring). It was a Masonic ring. (Swadell) said the Lord's prayer in Danish. The kid didn't know Danish from Latin."

It didn't matter. The lad went into battle feeling blessed. Swadell later used parts of the manual -- including a benediction from the Jewish section -- in his Protestant services.

"He liked it so much," she said.

Swadell died at 72 in 1968 after a long ministerial career. Shelton never knew the chaplain's manual existed, so she never wondered what happened to it, nor does she have a clue how it ended up for sale on eBay. She's glad it did, and that Calvez bought it.

Calvez, she's learned through their online discussions, is 43, has a tremendous respect for the American military and visits the cemetery at Normandy every year. He owns a Jeep, the license plate of which reads: 6.6.1944 D.Day Normandie. One room in his home is decorated with war memorabilia. But when he collects a war item that bears a name, such as Swadell's chaplain's manual, he tries to reunite it with the family.

Seeing the book when it arrived via FedEx last week brought her to tears -- even more so as she held it, opened it and saw the inscription.

"I saw my father's signature and realized he'd carried this in the war," she said, choking with emotion. "I loved getting it."

And she has Calvez, a perfect stranger with Internet service a half a world away, to thank.

Mary Rose Shelton died in 2015.

War hero grandpa inspires unlikely kinship

October 17, 2010

Grandpa was a war hero. Siblings Jack Merrill and Carol Anne Merrill Miller of Modesto knew that growing up.

They knew Col. Gyles Merrill, a stern and by-the-book career military man, chased Pancho Villa with Gen. John "Black Jack" Pershing in 1917. They knew Grandpa escaped World War II's horrific and heinous Bataan Death March in 1942 and organized guerrilla forces that harassed the Japanese army, softening it up for the Allied forces to retake the Philippines in 1944-45.

Bart Ah You / The Modesto Bee
Jack Miller, Paco Magsaysay and Carol Anne Merrill Miller.

And they knew their grandfather made a huge impact on the future of the Philippines when, as the war wore down, Gen. Douglas MacArthur asked him for a list of reliable Filipino citizens. One of them, MacArthur determined, would become the governor of the Zambales province. Merrill gave the general only one name: Ramon Magsaysay, who went on to become a congressman and then the third president of the Third Republic of the Philippines.

Col. Merrill died in 1954, a few months after Jack was born, and is buried at Arlington National Cemetery in Virginia. President Magsaysay died three years later in a plane crash just before he likely would have been re-elected for a second term. Two million people attended his funeral.

Magsaysay to this day remains a revered figure in the Philippines.

What Jack and Carol Anne didn't know until recently was how much the Magsaysay family and other Filipinos still revere their grandfather. Carol Anne got her first inkling when she wrote Magsaysay's son, Harvard-educated Ramon Jr., a letter in 2004 asking to know more about her grandfather's actions in the Philippines.

"I never expected an answer," she said.

Instead, she got a lengthy e-mail response from Ramon Jr., known as "Jun" Magsaysay. He also served in the Filipino Congress and Senate, retiring six years ago. Jun explained to her how Col. Merrill had launched his father's -- and ultimately his -- political career and how they considered him family. Thus, Merrill's family was also their family, and they wanted to meet Carol Anne and Jack someday. They didn't plan a visit, though, and lost contact.

Fast forward to April of this year, when Paco Magsaysay, Jun's son and grandson of the former president, was vacationing in the United States. He asked a friend to help him find the colonel's grandchildren. Before the friend could do so, Paco found Carol Anne on Facebook and messaged her. Her response? If he ever came to San Francisco, she and her brother would love to meet him and take him to dinner at Tomaso's, their favorite restaurant there.

"What are you doing next week?" Paco replied. They met and rekindled a friendship between two families, based upon a connection between their grandfathers that began six decades ago.

That morphed into an invitation for the Merrill grandkids – "kids" being misleading considering Jack is 56 and his sister is 55 -- to visit the Philippines in late August. They arrived in time to celebrate President Magsaysay's birthday, Aug. 31, which is a national holiday. They attended the annual Ramon Magsaysay Awards Foundation event, where they were guests of the Magsaysay family and sat alongside the ambassadors of Bangladesh and Saudi Arabia. They exchanged handshakes with current Philippine President Benigno Aquino III, who gave a stirring tribute to Ramon Magsaysay during the ceremonies.

"We had a delightful time," Jack said. "We were treated like visiting heads of state."

They enjoyed a 5½-hour lunch with Ramon Magsaysay's daughter, Mila Magsaysay Valenzuela. Jun Magsaysay told them their money was no good on this trip.

"I told Paco, 'Ask your father if we can take him to dinner,' " Jack said.

Paco text-messaged his father, who replied, "There's an old Chinese proverb that says, 'When you're the host, you're the host until the end.' Dinner's on me."

Last weekend, again in the United States, Paco Magsaysay came to Modesto to visit the Merrill family, and to tour dairy and almond operations. The 42-year-old has no political aspirations, at least at this point in his life. He owns a dairy and a cable television company in the Philippines.

Jack and Carol Anne plan to return to see the Magsaysays someday. They've enjoyed a windfall of unexpected opportunity, Jack contends.

"It's humbling," he said. "I feel like we're collecting a debt we didn't accrue. Jun told us, 'You're part of the family.' For them, it's very real. I absolutely feel the connection."

"It's been a wonderful thing for us," Carol Anne added.

They've gotten to know more about their heroic grandfather thanks to the devotion of a family a half a world away.

Bart Ah You / The Modesto Bee

Allen Sughrue, left, and Chuck Walker found out they were in the same Hungarian prison at the same time during World War II.

The bonds of war

Ex-POWs brought together decades later

July 8, 2007

They were shot down over Hungary five days apart during World War II. They both bailed out of their planes and were captured by some really mad Hungarians.

They were housed a floor or two apart in the same stone prison in Budapest, emerging with similar stories of bugs and bad culinary experiences.

They both endured long, forced marches from their respective German prison camps as the Russians surged in from the east.

And back home after the war, one worked for a company that made specialty bodies for trucks and the other became a truck mechanic.

Despite their parallel existences, Chuck Walker and Allen Sughrue didn't meet until Friday, when Sughrue moved into the Samaritan Village senior living complex in Hughson. Walker has lived there for the past 4½ years. "I have one big question," said Walker, who flew a P-38 fighter plane assigned to protect B-17 bombers such as the one from which Sughrue bailed. "What day were you shot down?"

Sughrue's plane went down July 2, 1944, another kill by a pack of German ME-109s five days before a 109 also sent Walker's crippled plane to the ground.

"We had mechanical problems and got all shot up," Sughrue said, then joked, "I was looking for you. Where were you?"

"This is going to take some time," Walker said, beaming.

They'll have plenty of it in the retirement complex -- time to compare their stories and rekindle their memories. Their kinship was immediate. The bonds of war supersede something so inconsequential as not really knowing each other. As they chatted, they learned their units both had been transferred from the North Africa campaign to an air base in Foggia, Italy, that had been captured from the Germans.

In his 11th mission in a B-17, Sughrue's plane had been damaged badly by the German planes while on a bombing run near Yugoslavia. He took shrapnel in his right leg.

"Three of them just shot us to pieces," he said.

Sughrue was the last of the crew to bail, staying behind to change his shoes and to make sure everyone else had gotten out.

"I free-fell at least 10,000 feet," Sughrue said. "I didn't want to get shot by the fighter planes while I was in a parachute."

He didn't pull the rip cord until he was about 5,000 from the ground, and landed in a grove of trees surrounded by a bog.

Five days later, Walker was shot down when his plane lost an engine, making him easy prey for an ME-109. He hit his head during the bailout, getting a concussion.

"I was knocked unconscious," Walker said. "I don't remember bailing out."

He somehow managed to pull the rip cord, and his parachute opened. As he hit the ground, he knew he wasn't much safer than he had been in the air.

"When I got my act together, I knew I had to get out of there," Walker said.

UNFRIENDLY CIVILIANS

He came upon a Hungarian farmer and thought that might be a good thing. Many times, the rural people helped downed American pilots. Those days of goodwill were over, as he learned when other Hungarians showed up.

"They were angry with me," Walker said. "They beat me up and knocked me unconscious again."

The finishing blow came when the flat side of a shovel whacked the side of his head. He was turned over to Hungarian authorities and taken to an abandoned airfield near Lake Balaton in central Hungary. He soon was joined by the crew of the downed B-17. One crewman had been poked in the back by a pitchfork-wielding farmer.

Finally, a Hungarian army captain explained the natives' hostility toward the Yanks: The Germans had convinced them that if the Americans won, they would kill the Hungarians' babies and rape their women.

"They believed them," he said.

Likewise, Sughrue incurred the wrath of the Hungarian locals.

"I tried to hide out until night, figuring I could work my way into Yugoslavia," he said. "The partisans were pretty good about helping us."

But the Hungarians combed the bog until they found him. Two of them were in-his-face screamers who wanted a lynching party.

"I missed being hung by about five minutes," Sughrue said. "Two Hungarian soldiers came and took me away from (the mob)."

After the village doctor cleaned his shrapnel wound, the soldiers took him to Budapest. There, the locals spat in his face and begged the soldiers to look the other way while they beat him to death, he said.

"I was thankful for those guards," Sughrue said.

He was taken to an old, four-story stone prison in Budapest and placed in a 6-by-10-foot cell on the second floor. His bed was a small wooden bench.

"The place was infested with bedbugs," Sughrue said. During the day, they hid in the brittle plaster on the walls.

"You could push on the loose stuff and blood would run out because you'd squished bedbugs," Sughrue said. "They were bloodsuckers."

He pulled the wooden bench away from the walls, making it tougher for the bugs to get to him at night.

"But you'd get a smart bedbug that would drop onto you from the ceiling," Sughrue said.

Walker was taken to the same prison and placed in a cell on the third or fourth floor. He said fleas were the problem there.

"They were horrendous," Walker said. "To pass the time, I'd count how many fleas I killed -- or how many bites were on me."

Both men said they were interrogated frequently by German officers, then returned to their solitary confinement cells.

"We had private rooms," Walker quipped. "We didn't have to share."

MYSTERY FOOD

They said the prison cuisine, if you could call it that, was pinch-your-nose edible at best. Sughrue, Walker and the other POWs survived on a diet consisting of a can of "some kind of liquid" for breakfast and boiled sugar beet tops for lunch. The one-course dinner?

"A barley soup with some kind of livestock floating in it," Walker said. "At first, I refused to eat it. But it wasn't long before you just ate whatever they brought you."

Walker stayed there less than a month before being put into a boxcar for a train ride to Stalag Luft III, southeast of Berlin. The camp primarily housed officers who were airmen. Walker was a second lieutenant. Events at Stalag Luft III, before Walker's arrival, became the basis for the movie "The Great Escape."

Despite Hitler's crackdown after the great escape, the British and Americans continued to run a radio station under the Germans' noses.

"We listened to the BBC every night," Walker said.

One POW stole the commandant's pet dachshund, he said.

"He'd tied (the dog) outside the barracks, and when he came back out, the leash and the collar were there, but the dog wasn't," Walker said. "Somebody had him for dinner."

Sughrue's stay at the Budapest prison lasted about six weeks before he was shipped to Stalag Luft IV, along the Baltic Coast.

MARCHING ORDERS

With the German military machine weakened by incessant pounding by Allied forces, the Russians moved west in February 1945. The Germans forced the POWs to march, trekking for 86 days in the harsh German winter. Sughrue figures he walked more than 600 miles, often backtracking as dictated by news of Allied troop movements. He crossed the Elbe River three times in a month.

Walker, meanwhile, went on an extended hike that took him into Vienna, Austria, where he briefly was held in a small prison.

"They put me in a cell, and I woke up with a rat on my face and a rat on my stomach," Walker said. "I'll bet that rat on my face is still in orbit."

From there, he marched to Frankfurt, sleeping in barns to stay out of the snow, and "liberating" whatever food he could find. He ultimately ended up in Stalag VII A in Moosburg, where tanks from Gen. Patton's 3rd Army came crashing through the fences to free the POWs.

Patton never was one to knock.

"Ten months almost to the day," Walker said, referring to the day he was captured.

Sughrue was in a village in northern Germany when a truck carrying British officers approached the POWs and told them the Allies had seized control of the area. They were now free.

Within weeks -- after getting deloused, new clothes and decent food -- both men were homeward bound on transport ships.

"There was never a day like the day we pulled into New York Harbor and there was that statue," Walker said.

Sughrue was disappointed that his ship went to Norfolk, Va., instead, depriving him of his own rendezvous with Lady Liberty.

That was a long, long time ago.

Friday, thanks to Samaritan Village officials who make it a point to know their residents, former POWs and coincidental prison mates Sughrue and Walker finally met.

They endured bullets and flak, the Hungarians, the Germans, vermin and malnutrition, and lived to tell about it.

"God was good to both of us," Walker said.

"I can't complain," Sughrue said. "We're here."

Sughrue lives in Hughson. Walker lives in Turlock.

Brian Ramsay / The Modesto Bee

Mark Perra, left, learned that the uncle he never knew died a noble death shortly after the D-Day invasion in 1944. Museum owner Tom Hillier worked with Perra to create a display at the Modesto City-County Airport honoring Walter Perra.

Bringing a hero to life

WWII pilot killed in France soars anew

May 3, 2009

To the people of a small area in northern France, he was an unknown American fighter pilot who gave his life rather than crash his burning plane into their village.

To the people of Modesto and certainly the vast majority of those now living in his hometown of Ceres, his is simply another name etched into granite monuments listing those killed in war -- memorialized but not really remembered.

And to his nephew, he was for decades more legend than real: the dashing and daring uncle who galloped horses, flew planes and died for his country.

Now, nearly 65 years after he died, Walter F. Perra has been brought back to life in fact, documents, lore, video and tribute. His memory will be honored Friday in a ceremony in the Les Corvées district of Vernouillet, France, where he died June 15, 1944.

Ceres native Mark Perra, the nephew born three years after Walter's death, will speak at the ceremony.

"I'm going back to thank this village for doing what we couldn't," Mark Perra said. On behalf of his family, he'll thank them for giving him a proper burial and for treating him as one of their own.

Walter Perra's story is one of bravery and sacrifice, no different from those of so many others who gave their lives during World War II and other wars. Perra's story, though, took decades to assemble even though he lived only 24 years.

Brian Ramsay / The Modesto Bee

Walter Perra's dogtags.

He grew up on the farm his parents, Richard and Ida Perra, owned at Service Road and Central Avenue. The third of four boys, Walter graduated from Ceres High in 1937. He studied aeronautics at Modesto Junior College and went to work designing aircraft fuel systems at Consolidated Vultee, which developed the B-24 Liberator bomber and other planes in Southern California.

Perra had two passions: flying planes and riding horses.

"I saw a pattern of Walter being drawn to where he's in control of really powerful animals and machines," Mark Perra said. "That's what he derived his joy from."

And what drove him from designing planes to flying them in combat.

"We're pretty sure Walter didn't have to sign up for pilot training," Mark Perra said. "He was in a critical position in a critical industry. I doubt he would have had to volunteer for the service, but that's what he wanted to do."

Walter joined the Army Air Corps to become a P-38 Lightning fighter pilot, completing his training in 1943. While at a base near Salinas, he once buzzed the family farm during a training run. Soon after, he steamed to England on the Queen Mary to join the 20th Fighter Group, 77th Fighter Squadron, based at King's Cliffe.

***

On June 6, 1944, Walter -- now a second lieutenant -- flew cover for bombers that pounded German gun placements and for the Allied soldiers trying to take the beaches at Normandy. He noted in his flight record, "June 6-7-8 -- flew fleet support, E-Channel (English Channel)."

As Allied forces moved inland, the flyboys attacked bridges and trains. Walter's onboard camera took remarkable film footage of him strafing a German supply train on June 14.

Flying at low altitude the next day, flak from German artillery tore into one of his engines, and it burst into flames. He knew his plane would crash, and the villages of Les Corvées, Dreux and Vernouillet loomed in his path.

"Some say he was about to crash in the village of Dreux and he may have stayed with his plane to guide (it) into a field nearby. In either case, at the last moment, he bailed out but was already too near the ground and was killed instantly about 100 yards from where his plane crashed," according to an account from French and American publications at the time.

German soldiers swept in to take his dog tags and flight jacket along with the plane's instruments and ID markings.

"(But) ... the mayor of the village preserved the plane number, 02104067, the plane was named 'Little Bug' and four swastikas were painted on the side," the report continued.

The information later enabled the Americans to identify Perra as the plane's pilot, and the swastikas likely represented his prior "kills" of German aircraft in his 18 missions.

For four days, the Germans, who still controlled the area, refused to let the locals bury this unknown pilot. And when they finally relented, the Germans refused to allow the French to bury him in a wooden casket.

Military historian Art Sevigny, who visited the region to research Perra's death, wrote that Vernouillet's mayor argued: "He is not a dog. You wouldn't bury your soldier that way."

The German commander finally allowed them to build the coffin. They marked Perra's grave with a small wooden cross bearing the day he died and adorned it with flowers. A group of children, four of whom had witnessed the crash, were among those who attended his funeral.

The following November, the Germans driven out, the villagers led Allied soldiers to the grave. His remains were moved to an interim military cemetery at St. Andres and then to the Normandy American Cemetery and Memorial at Colleville-sur-Mer, joining more than 9,000 other Americans buried near the beaches they died trying to take.

***

Back home in Ceres, the Perra family knew only that Walter had been declared missing. A day or so after receiving his MIA notification, they received a letter he had written shortly after the D-Day invasion. Not until Jan. 22, 1945, did they receive a personal letter from Gen. Hap Arnold informing them that Walter had been killed.

The family mourned, Mark Perra said, in a quiet and dignified way that muted their heartache. Over time, they received the dog tags the Germans had stripped from his body in 1944. They received his deceased soldier's file, which detailed every flight he took while in training and in battle. It included his medals, a Purple Heart among them.

"They collected stuff," Mark Perra said. "They didn't study it. It was too painful."

Mark Perra's father, Medrick Perra, kept it all, though.

"My parents (both now deceased) were pack rats," Mark said. "They saved everything."

***

While he often wondered about his uncle, it took a lucky break to get some real information about how Walter had died. In 2002, Mark Perra and his wife, Joanne, vacationed in France.

"We traveled to Normandy, and I believe it was the first time any family member had visited the grave site," he said.

A year later, he got a call from Sevigny, who was looking for relatives of Walter Perra. The American Battle Monuments Commission was preparing to build a new visitors center at the Normandy American Cemetery.

"They wanted to tell some of the stories of courage, competence and sacrifice of what it took to take that beach and move inland -- not through the eyes of the generals and strategists, but through the men who fought and died there," Mark Perra said. "They wanted to include an airman and found Walter Perra's story most intriguing."

Sevigny visited Les Corvées in 2005 and met with those who had been the children who witnessed the plane crash and attended Walter's funeral. Until then, the residents of the village never knew Walter's name, his hometown or anything else about him.

***

From Walter's file, Mark Perra discovered that when Walter's remains were taken from his original grave to St. Andres, his identity had not been confirmed.

"He was buried as Unknown X-121," Mark Perra said. "It was only later that Unknown X-121 was conclusively identified as Lt. Perra. ... In part, this accounts for the initiative to build a memorial for Walter now: (They) finally know who this person was."

As do those who enter the Normandy American Cemetery's visitors center, which opened in 2007. Guests watch "On Their Shoulders," a video that repeats every seven minutes.

Walter Perra is one of the men featured in the video, which, by pure coincidence, is narrated by Modesto native Harve Presnell.

The video's creator, Max Lewkowicz of New York, produced other videos that also feature Walter Perra. One of them, called "Sacrifice," includes footage Mark Perra came across while sifting through his uncle's belongings.

"I found this steel tin -- a large, round tin," Mark Perra said. "Inside were a whole bunch of rolls of 8-millimeter movies. They hadn't been looked at for 60 years."

Lewkowicz sent them to the National Archives to be digitized and preserved.

"There was film of (Walter) flying (near Modesto), the skies just as clear and clean and blue as you could imagine," said Mark Perra, who now lives in the East Bay. "There were shots taken on the family farm. Where there were open fields are now buildings and trees and development. The barn is gone now. It's striking how different it was."

The family's address -- Route 1, Box 152 -- is directly across the street from Ceres' newest high school, Central Valley.

***

Much of the Walter Perra memorabilia -- including photos, letters, high school yearbooks and military records -- is on display at Tom Hillier's museum at Modesto Airport. The museum houses a Boeing Stearman PT-13B plane that Walter Perra very likely flew while training at the Cal-Aero Academy in Ontario in the 1940s. Hillier and Mark Perra became friends because of Walter.

"We all have grown to think we know Walter from knowing this guy right here," Hillier said, pointing to Mark one recent afternoon. "There's a piece of Walter in Mark."

Mark and Joanne Perra soon will leave for France to attend the unveiling of a monument in his uncle's honor and to thank the people who built it. Among them will be the four children -- now adults in their 70s -- who witnessed Walter's death and helped protect his remains.

Nearly 65 years later, the villagers finally can call him by name. His family finally understands how he died.

And nephew Mark Perra -- Mark Walter Perra -- knows his uncle, even if they never met.

Mark Perra lives in Danville. Tom Hillier died in 2016.

WWII Navy veteran survives on sheer luck

May 25, 2007

William Davis has always had a unique sense of timing.

As a barber aboard the heavy cruiser USS Chester during World War II, the former Sonora and Modesto resident steamed into Pearl Harbor on Dec. 8, 1941, the day after the Japanese attacked. Rough seas had slowed the cruise into port.

"We were supposed to have been there, tied up for the admiral's inspection," Davis said.

Bart Ah You / The Modesto Bee
William Davis, with wife Helen, at VA Facility in Livermore.

During a patrol two months later, a Japanese bomb struck the ship's main deck, killing eight and wounding 38. Davis was assigned to an antiaircraft battery near the front of the ship and escaped injury. Then, the Chester arrived at the Battle of Midway just hours after the Japanese fleet had endured the beating that swung the war in the Pacific toward the Americans' favor.

"(Midway) was over before we got there," he said.

And while the Chester patrolled near the Solomon Islands later in 1942, it took a torpedo midship. Eleven men died and 12 were wounded. Again, Davis managed to escape without injury.

"It knocked a hole in that ship," Davis said. "A big hole. It hit directly underneath where I was standing."

Yes, life often comes down to timing, and Davis' manifested itself in different ways after he left the service.

His first wife, Helen Louise Davis, died in the same year -- 1981 -- as the husband of the woman who eventually became his second wife, Helen Marie Evans Davis.

Davis and Helen Marie spent 16 years together before marrying in 2000, waiting all those years because of financial and health care considerations, she said.

HATES ORDINARINESS OF THE PLACE

By 2001, his hearing was worsening from damage caused by the noise of the guns aboard the Chester. His arthritic hands grew more painful, and he suffered several strokes. He went to live at the veterans' retirement home in Livermore.

Now, their story is one of love and timing, and particularly the time they can spend together. Helen, who lives in Modesto, makes the drive over the Altamont twice weekly to be with him, saddened he can no longer walk and she is no longer physically strong enough to care for him at home.

At the same time, she is happy for the years they've shared. Helen is 82. Bill turned 90 on Friday, with about 25 family members and friends celebrating with him at the retirement home in Livermore.

"He's my friend, my playmate and my lover," Helen Davis said. "I was 58 when we got together and he was 65. At our ages, we didn't think we'd have all that long together. But God has been very good to us. He's given us all these years together."

Bill Davis said he hates the place. But it's not the facility, and certainly not the staff, whom Helen Davis said treats her husband wonderfully. Like so many of his generation, he simply hates that his declining health has taken away his independence and taken him away from his wife. Being in a retirement home is simply too ordinary, and Bill Davis' life has been anything but ordinary.

He became a barber in the Navy, assigned to cut only officers' hair. His other duty? Wearing asbestos gloves, he caught the hot shells ejected from anti-aircraft guns and threw them overboard.

Then, after leaving the Navy in 1947, he continued as a barber in civilian life. Work in a typical barbershop on a side street or in a strip mall? Not a chance.

GOLD RUSH-ERA BARBERSHOP

Among his stops, he ran the Pioneer Barber Shop in Columbia State Historic Park for 23 years.

"I was only the third barber in the history of that shop," he said.

He dressed the part, donning Gold Rush-era clothing, including a top hat popular at the time.

"My (first) wife worked in the New York Dry Goods store next door," Davis said. She also dressed in 1800s garb, as do many of those who work in the shops at the park.

He frequently played his banjo for customers and tourists in the state park.

Whenever Hollywood came to Tuolumne County to film movies -- as it has frequently -- Davis hired on as an extra. Among his films: "The Apple Dumpling Gang Rides Again" and "The Last Ride of the Dalton Gang," both filmed in 1979.

And about 10 years ago, Davis suddenly began getting calls from some folks who wanted to express their condolences.

He, or someone with the same name and age, had been listed in a death notice in an area newspaper. Mark Twain, who once lived a few miles away at Jackass Hill, once wrote, "The report of my death was an exaggeration."

So was Davis'.

"We had friends calling us," Helen Davis said. "We got it straightened out."

Bill Davis is still with us - still sharp enough to recall his war stories and his fortunate timing in life. His wife loves to hear his stories, no matter how many times he tells them.

Because while each story might center on his lucky timing, she focuses purely on their time together.

Bill Davis died in 2008.

Honors past due

History learned, son goes on quest

January 11, 2007

Many times before, Bill Moreno tried to get his father to sort through his military records and papers.

He wanted to understand what Ventura "Ben" Moreno experienced during World War II. He wanted the family, particularly the grandkids, to know about their grandpa's exploits.

But so like many of his era, Ben Moreno had endured too much to want to talk about it.

Ted Benson / The Modesto Bee
Ben Moreno with wife, Blanche, and son, William.

"He'd say, 'I served,' " Bill Moreno said. "Little bits and pieces came out, but that was about it."

It wasn't until eldest son Thomas took him back to Okinawa -- where Ben was wounded in 1945 -- in April 2006 that it all came to the surface.

"I got so emotional that a couple of times, I had to excuse myself," the 83-year-old Patterson man said.

Shortly after the trip ended, he decided yes, it was time to go through his military stuff and share his stories.

"We found his discharge papers and found that he had these medals coming," Bill Moreno said.

Six, actually: A Bronze Star, a Purple Heart, one for good conduct, one for serving in the Asiatic-Pacific campaign, another for serving in the American campaign and a World War II victory medal.

Ben Moreno never received them -- not even the Purple Heart he earned for being shot in the wrist. So son Bill set about trying to right that wrong.

His father finally will be honored during an invitation-only dinner Saturday night at the Diablo Grande Winery and Resort. An Army colonel from Sacramento will present Moreno's medals. He'll also be recognized by the city of Patterson for his activism, and by the Stanislaus County Sheriff's Department for his years as a citizen volunteer. Proceeds will benefit Modesto's Disabled Veterans organization.

All this will happen, in no small part, because son Bill made the effort to validate his father's military career, of which the Army had no record.

Like thousands of others, Ben Moreno's records were destroyed in 1973, when a warehouse at the National Personnel Record Center in St. Louis burned to the ground. Soldiers discharged from the Army from Nov. 1, 1912, to Jan. 1, 1960, simply didn't exist in the eyes of the military unless they had documents to prove their service. Same for Air Force personnel from Sept. 25, 1947, until Jan. 1, 1964.

Consequently, the military relies on families to provide documents needed to rebuild its databases and restore service records. Bill Moreno sent the Army copies of his father's documents, which now constitute Ben Moreno's permanent record. And he requested the medals his father deserves.

The Army responded quickly, by its own bureaucratic standards, in recognizing Moreno's service and providing the medals.

Finally, Ben Moreno's family is learning about his time overseas -- stories of how he was drafted in 1943 and rose to the rank of staff sergeant in the 10th Army's 184th Infantry Division. He's told them about missions on Okinawa, the last major campaign before the United States dropped atomic bombs on Japan to force the war to an end. These are stories he kept to himself for more than six decades. A few of them:

As the Americans planned one assault, Moreno said, a lieutenant told him to summon a medic.

"Then, he (the lieutenant) turned around and fell over," Moreno said. "He'd been shot from one side through the other by a Japanese sniper."

That gave an even greater urgency to their assignment.

"I was ordered to take my men and go blow up caves (where the snipers hid)," Ben Moreno said. "We were going to have to cross a ravine. The Japanese were above us with mortars."

One soldier refused to go.

"He said, 'You're the leader. You go ahead,' " Moreno said. "I told him, 'I have to make sure all of you get across.' "

Before they made their move, another young soldier handed Ben Moreno his ring, watch and wallet "because he thought something was going to happen."

They started across the ravine under a hail of bullets and mortars. "Anybody who tells you they weren't scared was a liar," Moreno said. "But you have to get it out of your mind. (As a squad leader) you're closer to your men than to your own brothers."

When the squad returned, some soldiers were surprised to see Ben Moreno. They thought he had been killed.

Instead, the only casualty was the young soldier who had given Moreno his belongings and predicted his own death. When they later found his body, it was stripped naked and the Japanese soldiers -- as they often did -- had pulled out his gold-filled teeth.

On another duty, Moreno and a fellow soldier went at 2 a.m. to wipe out an enemy machine gun nest.

"We were walking slowly or crawling most of the way," he said. "Out of the corner of my eye, I spotted the flash of machine guns. I hit the kid and knocked him down, and we crawled the rest of the way."

They tossed their grenades into the pit, killing the Japanese soldiers, and returned to camp. Only then did Moreno notice a numbness in his wrist.

"A bullet had gone right through it," he said. He spent six weeks in a Honolulu hospital. "A doctor told me the hand would be more or less paralyzed, but I told him no, I was going to use it."

Moreno soon began squeezing a rubber ball to strengthen the muscles, and regained use of the hand. When Moreno wouldn't put in for the Purple Heart, the doctor did so for him. But it never arrived, even though it was listed on his discharge papers.

In fact, Moreno never pursued any of the medals even though superiors recommended him for the honors. For any number of reasons, he never received them and would never have gotten them if not for his son's diligence.

It's the least a son could do, Bill Moreno said.

"It's something that he held in all this time."

The Morenos live in Tracy.

Veteran was in 1st Cavalry when they actually rode horses

November 11, 2006

The 1st Cavalry Division is the United States Army's largest, with more than 17,000 soldiers, and a vast array of armored vehicles and weaponry.

Turlock's Charlie Perrien, though, remembers when the term "cavalry" carried the image of soldiers on horseback, carrying only their rifles, bedroll and rations. The 87-year-old veteran was among the last horse soldiers who served in 1st Cavalry's 7th Regiment patrolling the Mexican border into World War II.

Marty Bicek / The Modesto Bee
Charlie Perrien was in the "real" Cavalry.

His unit represented the final remnant of the Army's tradition in the Old West -- one that began by protecting settlers and wagon trails in the 1860s. It continued with Gen. John J. "Black Jack" Pershing and a young lieutenant named George S. Patton unsuccessfully pursuing Pancho Villa into Mexico. Horses pulled American artillery in Europe during World War I.

The era of the horse cavalry ended, quite unceremoniously, in December 1942 when the Army deemed Perrien's unit would be more valuable on foot in the Pacific Theater.

"We came off the border and

they told us to turn in our horses," Perrien said.

Two months later, the horse soldiers of the 7th Regiment became infantrymen and were shipped to Australia.

Perrien grew up on a farm in Iowa and was drafted into the Army in October 1941.

"I'm the only one of seven boys who went into the service, and God blessed me," he said. "I'm the only one who's left out of the seven."

He and a buddy, inducted at the same time, thought they'd ask for cavalry duty. The decision already had been made for them, as they learned when they saw their names on the duty bulletin.

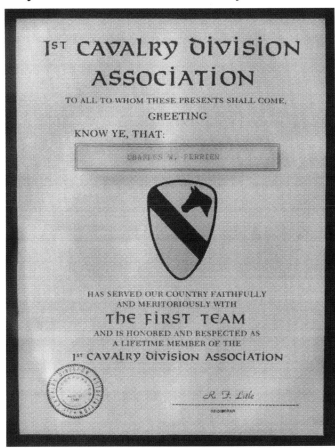

Marty Bicek / The Modesto Bee
Charlie Perrien's Cavalry certificate.

"I had this corporal who didn't think I knew anything about horses," Perrien said. "But I'd worked with horses all my life. On the farm, when I'd unhitch 'em and bring 'em back to the barn, I'd put one foot on each's back and ride 'em in Roman style."

He and girlfriend Jean were married secretly during a three-day leave shortly after he joined the Army. She worked for the phone company, which wanted only single women to preserve the stability of its work force.

"I'd have been fired if they knew I'd gotten married," Jean Perrien said. "I worked there for 14 months before he was transferred (to the infantry and shipped overseas)."

The young couple needed her income because he was still waiting for his first Army pay.

"She had to pay the preacher," Charlie Perrien said.

HORSES KNEW MORE THAN THEY DID

Likewise, the cavalry of the early 1940s had its rules. It was driven by procedures and regulations, and the soldiers did things strictly by the book or paid a price. Perrien's unit patrolled the Mexican border near El Paso, often staying out five to six weeks at a time. They watched for people trying to cross illegally into the United States. Returning to camp after a patrol one day, he noticed a commotion.

"Our horses had to eat before we did," Perrien said. "It took eight men to put a feedbag on a horse. By the time we got done eating, that horse was dead. There'd been a rattler in that feedbag. The horse knew it, and that's why he was fighting (the feedbag). Sometimes, the horses were smarter than we were."

Regulations also prohibited harsh disciplining of the animals.

"One guy got six months in the brig and six months with his pay suspended because he beat a horse with his .45 (-caliber pistol)," Perrien said.

He asked the commanding officer why the punishment was so severe.

"He told me, 'To get another GI, I just have to fill out the paperwork. To get another horse, they pay $275,' " Perrien said.

He did learn some survival skills, such as digging a pit to sleep in, to keep the cold night air from getting beneath him.

"If you were on top of the ground, you'd freeze to death," Perrien said.

Then, in December 1942, the order came down to disband the horse cavalry. Some of the horses, he believes, were sold to France for meat. Some were destroyed here, while others were given away to civilians.

Perrien and the others in his outfit were sent to Australia and then New Guinea. They eventually went on to the Philippines, where Perrien received five Bronze Stars liberating America prisoners of war under Gen. Douglas MacArthur while fighting on Leyte and Luzon.

"They showed that picture of (MacArthur) coming ashore," Perrien said with a laugh. "When they took it, we were already 20 miles inland."

He paid a personal price no medals could reward. Memories of emaciated Allied soldiers treated so inhumanely by the Japanese bothered him greatly, as did seeing other American soldiers lose their wits on the battlefields.

"The Japanese would counterattack at night," Perrien said. "I remember seeing our own guys go crazy and get out of their foxholes. They didn't get 40 feet before they were dead."

FIREPOWER AND HORSEPOWER

The events scarred him emotionally as well as physically, and he spent eight years after the war dealing with flashbacks and physical ailments. He returned to the United States weighing only 105 pounds. After being medically discharged in August 1945, he eventually became a buyer for the old Purity grocery chain. He and Jean moved to Turlock in 1968, buying 10 acres of peach orchards near Fulkerth Road. He also raised pheasants for hunting clubs, and stored most of his military memorabilia -- including his old cavalry uniform and some photographs -- in a steel building on the property. One day, his nephew called to tell him somebody had broken into the building and stolen the memorabilia. They later found the stuff in a pile, rotted by rain and not worth keeping, he said.

He has only a certificate showing he was in the 1st Cavalry, a portrait of himself in uniform, and his discharge papers.

The Army brought back the horse cavalry in 1972, but strictly as a public relations tool. It rides in parades, at rodeos and state fairs, with its soldiers staging drills and weapons demonstrations.

Today's 1st Cavalry is all about everything to do with manpower, firepower and horsepower, but not of the four-legged variety.

Perrien, though, remembers riding along the Mexican border in a McClellan saddle -- the last of the true American horse soldiers.

It's a rare veteran memory, indeed.

Charlie Perrien died in 2016.

Kamikaze survivor among us

September 1, 2005

Dan Donnelly bears the distinction of being the valley's oldest surviving World War II kamikaze pilot.

Huh? Wait a minute, you say ... a successful kamikaze pilot flew one mission, period. At least, that's the way it worked for the Japanese, whose kamikazes tried to crash their planes into U.S. warships.

By 1944, the United States held a huge technological edge over the Japanese, who lacked the material resources to replace their depleted war machinery. The United States, meanwhile, churned out planes, tanks, guns and warships, and developed new weaponry that was extremely sophisticated for the time.

The latter included top-secret drone planes -- piloted by remote control from trailing planes -- that attacked Japanese targets in the Pacific islands.

Donnelly, a longtime Oakdale resident and feed store owner who will turn 90 on Oct. 6, was a Navy trainer pilot selected to work in the program beginning July 4, 1943.

Adrian Mendoza / The Modesto Bee
Dan Donnelly was part of a top-secret drone program during World War II.

Two U.S. squadrons experimented with drones. One went to England to attack German submarine bases. The other – Donnelly's

-- went to the Pacific in 1944. The twin-engine drones were armed with 2,000-pound bombs and had television cameras in the nose cones.

The drone camera transmitted a picture to monitors in the trailing planes carrying Donnelly and his crewmen. They could release the bomb from the drone as it reached its target. But in many cases, they sacrificed the planes by crashing them into Japanese ships just as Japanese kamikazes attacked U.S. ships, but with one major difference.

"We didn't lose a single person," Donnelly said.

During one mission, he guided a drone to 50 feet above the surface of a bay on an island where Japanese gunners were targeting U.S. planes.

"(The Japanese) had guys out there in boats to shoot our pilots, who were bailing out after being shot down," he said. "We took 'em by surprise. We got our target."

It was clearly unusual duty in an unusual flying career for Donnelly.

Daniel Felix Donnelly was born in Oakland in 1915. When he was 6, his father -- Daniel Patrick Donnelly -- moved the family to Oakdale and settled on a ranch east of town near the Stanislaus River. They milked about 18 cows, but his father's best crop came out of a still: bootlegged whisky. During Prohibition, the elder Donnelly had friends among law enforcement who would warn him whenever the feds were headed his way.

"They raided him eight times and caught him only once," Donnelly said.

He graduated from Oakdale High School in 1933 and spent a year at Modesto Junior College. In 1935, he transferred to St. Mary's College in Moraga, living with relatives in Oakland and traveling by train to and from school each day. He left school after his father died suddenly that same year.

"I never went back," he said. "I stayed (in Oakdale), milked the cows and ran the ranch."

And he found his passion. One day, about a year after his father died, Donnelly heard a twin-engine plane coming in low over the ranch.

"It was at about 800 feet over Dad's place," Donnelly said. "I made up my mind that day that someday I'd learn to fly an airplane like that."

He answered a newspaper ad calling for young, single men who wanted to learn to fly. The catch was that if the United States went to war, they'd be called to service. Nowadays, they're called reserves.

Donnelly signed up, took the course, and the Navy summoned him to serve in the spring of 1941, sending him to Jacksonville, Fla., for flight training. Soon, the student became the instructor and was sent back to Oakland. He became the first pilot to land on a field that had just been cleared of barley -- part of 3,000 acres that the Navy purchased east of

Livermore. That naval air station later became the site of Lawrence Livermore National Laboratory.

Donnelly had married and started a family by the time the Navy selected him for the secret drone program in Clinton, Okla., and eventually sent him to the Pacific.

The drone project was cut short by a new secret weapon -- the atom bombs that would be dropped on Hiroshima and Nagasaki -- and Donnelly left the Navy in November 1945. Even so, the drone program remained classified for 16 years after the war ended.

Donnelly, meanwhile, returned to the valley and built what is now Oakdale Municipal Airport -- now called Dan Donnelly Field -- before selling his interest in the airfield and opening Oakdale Feed and Seed in 1950. Adding stores in Modesto, Madera and Sheldon (east of Elk Grove) took away his flying time, but he still dreams of one more flight.

"I want to mix a bourbon and coke, (parachute) out of a plane and drink it on the way down on my 90th birthday," he said, pointing out that former President Bush parachuted at age 80. "And I could do it, too. But my wife won't go for that."

Thus, the valley's oldest kamikaze pilot will have to settle for turning 90 on the ground, safe and sound.

Dan Donnelly died in 2010.

Luftwaffe ace's son gets glimpse into father's past

May 11, 2006

Fred Eichel's father didn't talk much about his experiences as a World War II fighter pilot.

Consequently, many stories died with him 10 years ago.

"He would say that he was sad about the people who had to suffer because of Hitler," Eichel said.

Courtesy of Fred Eichel
German fighter pilot Deet Eichel.

Eichel's dad, Diethelm von Eichel-Streiber, was a highly decorated ace in Germany's Luftwaffe. "Deet" Eichel flew the famous Messerschmitt Me-109 that controlled the European skies during much of the war. He was credited with 96 victories, mostly on the Eastern front.

Three times he was shot down behind enemy lines, only to sneak back to fly again. But while he was one of the country's top fliers, Deet Eichel never joined the Nazi party, never embraced its supremacist attitude. One of his uncles was among those who conspired, unsuccessfully, to assassinate Adolf Hitler in 1944.

When the war ended, Deet Eichel came to the United States and eventually settled in Modesto. He opened the city's first Volkswagen dealership in 1955.

Meanwhile, after the fall of the Third Reich, the Allies dismantled what remained of the German war machine. Most of the surviving Messerschmitts were scrapped. In fact, only seven still exist in the world, and only two in the United States can still be flown.

One of them will be in town Saturday for a show at the Modesto Airport. Fred Eichel, a real estate agent in Modesto, is among those paying pilot Skip Holm of southern California to bring the plane to Modesto.

"My goal is to sit in that plane and bring my kids -- his grandkids -to see what their grandfather did," Fred Eichel said.

So sometime before noon, Eichel and his family will watch Holm land and then get a much closer look. And perhaps they'll come to understand, after talking with Holm, how skilled Deet Eichel had to be to fly so many missions in a plane that always made landing an adventure.

"They lost 10,000 of these planes in landing accidents," said Holm, who has flown nearly every type of fighter plane ever made, including American P-51 Mustangs, Japanese Zeroes and Russian MiGs and Yaks.

The first Messerschmitt crash-landed on its maiden voyage in 1935, when the landing gear malfunctioned. That was just the first in a long history of landing issues with the plane.

"The problem wasn't in combat even though they were often outnumbered 100-to-1," he said. "It was landing it. You cannot let it get off even one or two degrees. If you do, you can't control it. If you don't have an iron cross (crisscrossing runways offering different wind directions) you don't want to even try (landing)."

The problem was that pilots had to control the plane with a rudder that was too small and thus ineffective, Holm said.

The Messerschmitt that Holm will fly to Modesto is owned by Harold Kingsvater of Fresno. Kingsvater resurrected the aircraft from the scrap heap.

"It was one of the airplanes that was in the movie 'D-Day,' " he said, referring to a 1994 film. "It got wrecked in the movie. Harold worked on it for 10 years to get it flying again."

Holm has logged more than 200 hours in the plane and jokes that he's now the "most experienced living Luftwaffe pilot in the world."

The plane's other downside is that it holds only enough fuel to fly about 300 miles, with a 695-horsepower Rolls-Royce Kestrel engine that generates a top speed of about 460 mph. That turns a cross-country trip into a series of short hops, Holm said.

"You barely get airborne and you're figuring out where you're going to land," he said.

But while in the air, the Messerschmitt was better than virtually any other fighter plane, "except maybe the (British) Spitfire," Holm said.

And that's where pilots such as Deet Eichel fought their battles during World War II. Yet, he seldom discussed his dogfights once he came to the United States, except in his final years, when his son captured about 12 hours of storytelling on videotape.

Modestans knew him mostly as a car salesman who made friends easily.

"My dad was an incredible human being," Fred Eichel said. "He loved people. He'd put on a cowboy hat, his black formal lederhosen (bibbed shorts) and cowboy boots, and called himself the German Okie. He was proficient on the accordion. He was a precious person."

And Saturday, Fred Eichel will get a bird's-eye glimpse into his late father's past.

Debbie Noda / The Modesto Bee
Fred Eichel in the cockpit of the Messershmitt ME-109, the same type of plane his father, German ace Deet Eichel, flew during World War II.

A real 5-star family during World War II

January 6, 2005

They were a five-star family -- four brothers and a sister who served in the U.S. military during World War II.

Robert Nicholson endured 30 straight days of zero-degree weather during the Battle of the Bulge on his way to earning five battle stars and a Purple Heart. Charles Nicholson survived a bullet in the groin fighting on Iwo Jima, and went on to a career spanning three decades in the Marines.

Roger Nicholson transported soldiers and supplies from troop carriers offshore to the island beaches of Iwo Jima, Guadalcanal, Guam and Saipan.

Helen Nicholson enlisted in the Marines and worked as a clerk in Virginia.

But because the three older Nicholson boys were in the thick of it, younger brother Dick Nicholson never saw the combat he so desired. After five brothers from Iowa died together when their ship was sunk in 1942, the military

Joan Barnett Lee / The Modesto Bee
Dick Nicholson with photos of himself and four siblings, all of whom served during World War II.

became hesitant to allow all the sons from the same family into combat at the same time. So Dick Nicholson, a Marine, was told he'd have to wait until one of his brothers returned to the States. By the time that happened, and Roger came home, the war had ended.

"To this day, I regret I wasn't sent over there," Dick Nicholson said. "I joined for a reason. I put in for aircraft carrier duty and battleship duty and was turned down for both. It's a feeling that's hard to describe. Everybody gets tested in life, and I wanted to see if I could take it."

Instead, his test came in the Alaskan cold after Japanese invaders were driven from Attu. He never fired upon an enemy. Still, few American families can boast of five children serving at the same time, as did the Nicholsons, and that bond very well could be what keeps the four brothers in touch today. Helen died three years ago.

"I'm very, very proud of them all," said Robert Nicholson, 85 and living in Green Valley, Ariz.

The Nicholson family moved to the valley in the winter of 1929-30, settling on a ranch east of Stockton. Their parents eventually divorced.

"We were scattered around with different relatives," said Roger, 84, who lives in Stockton. "We weren't living together as a family. The Great Depression wasn't really over. (The military) was a godsend for all five of us. We all walked into pretty good jobs."

Robert entered the Army in 1941, eight months before Pearl Harbor.

"Anybody with an ounce of sense saw we were going to war," said Robert, who fought at Normandy, Remagen and into Berlin with Gen. George Patton's 3rd Army.

Charles, Roger and Helen then joined the Marines. Dick, the only Nicholson boy to graduate from high school, joined in 1943.

Roger and Charles, both in the Marines' 3rd Division, spent the entire war in the Pacific campaign and actually met up on Bougainville.

"I'd been rolling barrels of gasoline," Roger said. "It was so humid. I was sitting on a coconut (tree) log, exhausted. A group of guys came marching by, and I looked up and one of them said, 'Hi, Roger.' I said, 'Hi, Chuck.' The guy sitting next to me asked, 'Who's that?' 'It's my brother,' I told him."

When the war ended, Charles stayed in the Marines and fought in Korea and Vietnam before retiring as a lieutenant colonel in 1970. Now 83, he lives in San Diego.

Robert stayed on in Europe to help formerly enslaved Poles, Czechs and Slavs return to their homes before he returned to the States and worked for Union Oil. Roger came home and was deer hunting near Lake Alpine when a bullet whizzed past his head and into a piece of granite that shattered, pieces nicking him in the eye.

"I'm thinking, here I made it through three years of war and almost get killed hunting deer," said Roger, who went to work for San Joaquin County. "I sold my rifle and never hunted again."

And Dick Nicholson finally saw action in the battle of Tucson -- as a pitcher in the Class A Arizona-Texas League. He went 12-9 in 1947, followed by an 8-1 start the next season. But he was wounded when a projectile -- in the form of a line drive -- struck his pitching shoulder.

"Ended my career right then and there," said Dick, 81. He worked as a radio announcer in Modesto, where he still lives, for years before managing the leasing and rental department of a car dealership.

The brothers get together whenever they can, including a reunion in Arizona last fall -- the remaining four from an American five-star family.

"I remember my brother Rob saying, 'We have the greatest country in the world, and I'm proud to serve it,' " Dick Nicholson said. "We all felt the same way."

Dick Nicholson died in 2013.

Marty Bicek / The Modesto Bee
Bobby Rommel displays medals that arrived 60 years after he earned them.

Medals presented 6 decades late

July 13, 2004

War heroes aren't supposed to pin on their own decorations.

Military protocol dictates that someone else -- a superior officer, a politician or some other high-ranking person -- is supposed to do that for them. After all, when you go to war and risk your life for your country, the circumstances merit the pomp.

For a number of reasons, Modesto's Bobbie Jack Rommel received his Purple Heart, Distinguished Service Medal, Good Conduct Medal, the Presidential Unit emblem, the World War II victory emblem and combat infantry badge nearly 60 years late and in a manila envelope.

No salute, no shaking of hands, no flags waving in the breeze. That changed Saturday night, when the 80-year-old Rommel got his long-overdue ceremony during a surprise gathering in Modesto.

Surprised? When he arrived at neighbor Cathie Carter's central Modesto home, he noticed the many cars parked along the street. He mentioned that it looked like someone was having a party.

"Uh ... yeah," muttered Carter, who orchestrated the event.

Even after Rommel entered the yard to find about 80 friends and relatives waiting, he wasn't immediately sure of what to make of it.

"I looked around and I thought, 'Where's the barbecue?' She (Carter) said she was having a barbecue."

Then he saw his five children, including daughter Cheri Silva, who flew in from Brazil. The retired building contractor saw many friends, including fellow WWII veteran and childhood buddy Harold Stedman of Modesto. Rommel figured something else was up. After all, your average backyard barbecue generally doesn't include U.S. Rep. Dennis Cardoza and an honor guard.

Rommels moment was finally at hand, so fitting and so appropriate for a man who had waited so long.

Drafted by the Army in 1943, Rommel volunteered for paratrooper duty and was assigned to the 101st Airborne.

"I flew in a plane 18 times before I landed in one," he said.

His unit went to England for extensive training in destroying pillboxes -- the concrete bunkers used by German soldiers as they fired on Allied troops. After a pep talk by Gen. Dwight D. Eisenhower, Rommel's unit flew out of southern England toward Normandy, arriving just a few minutes into June 6, 1944.

"I was 19 years old," Rommel said. "I figured if I made it to be 20, which was two days after we jumped, I'd make it. Before we left, the chaplain came to the staging area and asked if anybody wanted to be baptized. I said, 'Now is as good a time as any.' "

The assault on Normandy began, and the German officer in charge of defending Normandy was a shirttail relative, Field Marshal Erwin Rommel, the notorious "Desert Fox."

"He was my dad's second cousin," Rommel said.

Rommel -- Bobbie Jack, that is -- survived tracers and machine gun fire to reach the ground alive.

"I never remember being scared," he said. "I always felt like I had a shield -- my guardian angel was the best in the world."

He later parachuted into Holland before being trucked to the Battle of the Bulge, where a chunk of shrapnel pierced his left foot. He spent 119 days healing in an English hospital as the European campaign neared its end. While others in his regiment received their medals, he was detached from the unit because he could no longer jump out of airplanes.

"They sent me back to France," he said. "I drove a truck for a USO troupe."

Yet another irony: The war was now over and a bunch of show biz hams routinely took their bows after entertaining the troops while he still hadn't gotten so much as an official "thank you."

In fact, Rommel waited nearly six decades to get most of his medals (he's still missing a few). Then-Rep. Gary Condit's staff diligently pursued the issue in 2001.

"He was going to give me my medals himself," Rommel said. "But he got himself into that mess." (Condit lost his re-election bid in 2002, mired in controversy over his relationship with Chandra Levy, the Modesto woman whose murder in Washington, D.C., remains unsolved.)

Instead, the medals came in that envelope.

Saturday's ceremony brought some closure. Condit's successor, Cardoza, and representatives from the city and state participated. They read proclamations, explained what Rommel did to earn his medals and honored this war hero. Finally, it became official, just as it should have been 60 years ago.

Bobby Rommel died in 2009.

Veterans' memories soar back with the roar of B-29 bomber Fifi's engines

September 9, 2016

Ralph Aquaro turned and smiled as the four engines of the B-29

Jeff Jardine / The Modesto Bee
Inside the B-29 "Fifi" as it landed in Modesto.

Superfortress named Fifi rumbled to life and the World War II-era bomber taxied out to the runway Monday morning in Monterey.

Aquaro is no kid with a simple fascination with big planes with big engines that make big noises, even though the Fifi – one of only two B-29s still flying – certainly commands the awe accorded to the big old warbirds.

He's 96 years old, and his fascination, like that of Modesto's Sam Satariano, comes from vivid memories of the plane's sounds and smells that returned when they rode as guests of the Commemorative Air Force and its AirPower History Tour. In fact, Aquaro and Satariano represent the very history the nonprofit organization wants to preserve as it takes the Fifi from city to city across the nation.

These men and former B-29 bombardier Hank Adams of Turlock – who at 92 can no longer get into the plane but came to the airport to spur his recollections as well – are among the last of a generation that soon won't be around to tell their stories of what it was like to fly B-29s in wartime. It's the same type of plane as the Enola Gay and the Bockscar, which dropped the atomic bombs on Hiroshima and Nagasaki to end World War II.

With Aquaro and Satariano aboard, the Fifi arrived in Modesto for five days of public tours, educational events and pay-for rides that enable the B-29, a C-45 Expeditor and a T-6 Texan – the latter being World War II training aircraft – to keep flying and teaching. Beginning Wednesday on the airport's general aviation side, hundreds of people including student groups will see the planes up close and personal, getting an understanding of the types of machinery that helped win World War II in ways no school textbook could possibly match.

Nobody gets more from hearing the stories of those who flew these planes during wartime than the crew flying the aircraft now, said Mark Novak, who piloted the Fifi into Modesto as he did during a similar visit in 2014.

"We learn a lot from the old guys," he said. "A lot of them tell us we do it wrong. But we operate the plane differently, we tell them, because there is only one (two after another, called Doc, in July returned to the skies for the first time since 1956). So we do a lot of things more safely."

And, of course, today's crew isn't facing anti-aircraft flak or enemy fighter planes looking for a big score. Neither man had ridden in a warplane since leaving the military decades ago. Aquaro served as a radioman on the crew of the Caboose, a B-29 crew he said concentrated most of its efforts on bombing the Mariana Islands. The plane also flew the last B-29 mission of World War II, attacking Japan roughly six days after the United States dropped the second of two atomic bombs in August 1945.

"We bombed a fuel refinery in Sapporo," Aquaro said. "We were supposed to be at 35,000 feet, but we dropped down to 15,000. We hit it, and flames came up all around us. Then, on our way back to Guam, I radioed San Francisco and they said the war was over. (The Japanese) had capitulated."

Satariano flew 25 missions as a B-17 pilot over Europe, thinking it would be fun until he encountered his first resistance bombing German installations in the Rhine Valley.

"You'd look down and see what looked like ants on the runways," he said. "It was fighter planes scrambling to get up and after you. Suddenly, the sky was black from (anti-aircraft) flak. And I'm thinking, 'What the hell have I gotten myself into?' I wanted to get out of the Air Force as fast as I could."

Instead, he trained to fly B-29s stateside as the war ended and then left the service. Soon after, though, he was called back to fly C-54s loaded with supplies into Germany during the Berlin Airlift. When the airlift ended in 1949, he again left the Air Force.

"Six months later, though, they called me back in again for the Korean War," he said.

A Modesto native who still lives on property his family has owned for nearly a century, Satariano went to Randolph Air Force Base in Texas to train B-29 pilots. Suddenly, his orders changed.

"They were going to send us to combat in Korea," Satariano said. "I looked at the colonel and asked him, 'Have you ever been in combat?' He said, 'No.' I said, 'I thought we were supposed to replace you here (in training) and you were supposed to go to combat.' "

When the colonel told Satariano it didn't work that way, Satariano told the officer he'd be calling his congressman to see about that.

"The next day, they sent me to Castle (Air Force Base in Merced)," he said.

Which he flew over Monday in the Fifi.

"Beautiful country," Satariano said. "A beautiful ride."

Adams, the bombardier who couldn't make the flight, stared out from the shade of the hangar at the plane as it rested, bomb bay doors open, on the tarmac.

"That bomb bay brings back memories," he said. "It reminds me of the time I had to go down into the bomb bay and release a bomb by hand. We couldn't land with it in there. That happened to another plane and it blew up (on landing). The (B-29) amazed me. It weighed what, 145,000 pounds loaded and 80,000 pounds empty. And it still got off the ground."

Aquaro, meanwhile, remembers training in Grand Island, Neb., to become a radio operator. The Philadelphia resident met his future wife, Corrine, there, and they made their life together after the war in Manteca, moving later to Ripon, where they lived until her death in 2009. At 96, he still works maybe a day a week at the automotive electrical business he started five decades ago and that his sons still run.

His trip on the Fifi gave him the opportunity to do what he never did as a B-29 crew member. He sat up front in the bombardier's seat in the nosecone instead of the radio operator's seat further back near where a gun turret once had been.

"I remember it being really crowded with that central firing service there," he said. The bombardier's seat? Now that was eye-opening, particularly when pilot Novak took the plane through a cut between mountains near Pacheco Pass.

"We never flew so close to the ground," he said.

When the plane rolled to its stop in Modesto, family and others greeted these men as if the war had just ended and they were returning heroes. And they were, returning to their pasts with high-flying flashbacks – of the sounds and smells of the old warbirds so few others could possibly own.

An hour in the sky rekindled their fascination with the B-29 and the memories of a lifetime.

Jeff Jardine / The Modesto Bee
B-29 bomber "Fifi" in Monterey before flight to Modesto.

Ralph Aquaro lives in Ripon and still drops by the electrical shop he owns. Sam Satariano lives in Modesto.

Courtesy of The Modesto Bee

Frank Alvarez honored the Aztec Eagles by visiting them in Mexico and hosting them in Modesto through the American GI Forum.

Vet goes to salute Aztec Eagles

November 11, 2003

Frank Alvarez knew of Escuadron 201.

He'd met some of its surviving members over the years at various American GI Forum functions.

But until the 49-year-old Modestan and Air Force veteran was invited to next week's reunion of the squadron's surviving members, he never really understood the extent of their contribution during World War II.

"I didn't know any of the details of what they had done until I pulled it up on the Internet," said Alvarez, a gang crime prosecutor for the Stanislaus County district attorney's office.

In fact, few Americans -- including Hispanic-Americans -- are aware of the role the squadron played in the Pacific campaign during the war's final summer.

When Nazi U-boats torpedoed and sank a pair of Mexican ships in May 1942, Mexico joined American and Allied efforts by declaring war on the Axis powers of Germany, Italy and Japan.

For the most part, history books have regarded the bracero program as Mexico's only major contribution to the war effort. Because it had no well-trained army, the Mexican government sent workers, called braceros, north to work in the fields and orchards in the United States to keep the food supply going.

Then, in 1944, Mexico sent 38 pilots and about 260 crewmen to be trained at military bases in Texas, Idaho and California. They formed the Mexican Expeditionary Air Force, known as the Aztec Eagles.

The pilots and support personnel shipped out to the Philippine Islands in May 1945, becoming the only Mexican military unit to fight in the war. From June 4 to Aug. 8, those pilots combined to fly 59 combat missions totaling 1,290 hours. They dropped 538 1,000-pound bombs, 500 500-pounders and strafed the Japanese with nearly 153,000 .50-caliber rounds.

Five of the 31 pilots who flew combat missions were killed in action as the Allies stepped up the pressure on dwindling Japanese air forces.

After they helped knock Japan out of the sky, some members of Escuadron 201 saw duty as ground support troops.

The fighting ended in early August, and the Japanese formally surrendered Sept. 2, 1945.

The squadron and its members were honored by President Truman and Gen. Douglas MacArthur before being welcomed home as national heroes in Mexico on Nov. 18, 1945.

Only 10 of the 300 squadron members, including highly decorated Capt. Reynaldo Gallardo, are still living. Every Nov. 18, the survivors meet to remember their compadres and remind Mexican citizens of their role in the war.

They found an ally in the American GI Forum, which started as a group of Hispanic-Americans who, Alvarez said, didn't receive the same treatment accorded other U.S. military veterans. The group is now open to all veterans regardless of heritage.

"What's exciting is that they (the Aztec Eagles) have come to our conferences in the past," Alvarez said. "Now we get to go to one of their celebrations of what they accomplished in World War II."

Alvarez, who will attend the Mexican celebration with his wife, Sandra, isn't sure what kinds of stories he'll hear from the Escuadron 201 pilots next week.

"When you're in a veterans group or at a conference, for whatever reason, you don't go into what you did," he said. "You know what branch they were in -- the Mexican air force or whatever. They talk about the basic training, the food and things like that."

They seldom tell combat stories, he said. No matter how heroic their exploits, veterans tend to maintain a solemn respect for those, ally or enemy, who died serving their country.

Today in Modesto and across the nation, Alvarez and others can bask in the glory of being an American military veteran -- the flag waving, the parades.

Then he'll go to Mexico to applaud the members, living and dead, of Escuadron 201.

"It will be a big honor to honor them," he said.

Frank Alvarez, a veteran and Stanislaus County Deputy District Attorney, died in 2012.

Miss Davis and WWII get in way of diploma

December 23, 2003

Modesto's Dave Cummings finally has his high school diploma, and Miss Davis, he admits, wouldn't have liked it one bit.

After all, he failed to turn his book report in on time, and she was stickler for such things.

So in the spring of 1942, the stern and unbending teacher at Michigan's Ypsilanti High School declared Cummings ineligible to participate in extracurricular activities.

That meant Cummings, a senior and the swimming team's best diver, couldn't compete in the Michigan state meet the following week. It meant Ypsilanti High would fall 10 points shy of winning the state swimming title -- points he likely would have generated through medals in diving and on a relay team.

And it ultimately meant he wouldn't receive his high school diploma -- for 61 more years. Just three months before graduation, Cummings quit high school. He enlisted in the army and served as a medic in Europe throughout the remainder of World War II.

He saw the horrors of battle that, for many years, made lacking his high school diploma seem pretty insignificant.

"I got as much education as anyone else," said Cummings, 81. "But I always wished I'd have gotten my diploma."

It remained that way until last month, when the school's board of trustees voted to award diplomas to its former students who went off to war before graduating. Cummings was the school's first to get his diploma in that manner.

Ironically, Cummings got it, in no small part, because he attended the 50th and 60th reunions of the class from which he failed to graduate.

"At the 60th (in 2002), he told me, 'I always wish I'd gotten my diploma,' " former classmate Austin Norton said. "And that got me to thinking."

Last month, Norton called with some good news.

"He said, 'Dave, I'm pretty sure we can get your diploma for you,'" Cummings said. "After all this time, I couldn't believe it."

On Nov. 24, 2003, the board finally granted David Cummings, Ypsilanti High, Class of 1942, his diploma.

Norton and three other former classmates accepted it on his behalf at a board meeting. Cummings received it in the mail after Thanksgiving.

"I knew they must have gone to an awful lot of trouble to get it," he said.

Their troubles were nothing compared to what the dreaded -- and long-ago deceased -- Miss Davis put Cummings and other students through, Norton said.

"She stopped a lot of kids back then," he said.

Several people, including other students, pleaded with the teacher to let Cummings finish the report and turn it in late. The more they urged her, the harder she resisted.

"David had an eye problem that made reading and studying tough," Norton said.

Miss Davis refused to give in.

"She was tough on everybody," said Cummings, who keeps busy by working part-time at Jack Tone Golf in Ripon. "The coach went in and tried to talk to her. He said, 'Sure, punish him, but not now.' But she wouldn't listen to anyone. The timing of it was awful."

Embarrassed and angry, Cummings said he tossed his books into a corner and walked out.

He got married after the war and raised four children. Cummings distributed newspapers in Arizona and California before becoming a merchant marine. His wife, Virginia, died in 1968. He later met a Korean woman during his travels.

"We were married in the embassy over there," he said.

They moved to Modesto when he retired in 1980. His second wife, Kuni, now suffers from Alzheimer's Disease and is in a care facility in Turlock. About two years ago, Cummings began working at the golf course, opening in the mornings and playing for free in the afternoons.

He's met other World War II veterans who play there. They talk about their golf games and swap war stories. But they can't match his graduation tale -- what it cost him, how it changed his life when he didn't turn in a book report on schedule, and how he finally got his diploma.

"It was my fault," Cummings said. "No question about it. I should have gotten it done. But it was bad timing for punishment."

Sixty-one years, to be exact.

David Cummings died in 2014.

Memories of war, trials still vivid

May 27, 2012

During an 18-month span beginning in July 1944, Robert W. Gilbert went from the tennis courts of **Modesto** High School to the courtroom of the **Nuremberg** war crimes trials, and was changed forever by his experiences.

Because, in that small window of his life, Gilbert endured a range of emotions he can vividly recall today: fear, confusion, pain, sadness, disgust and joy. These memories remain and resurface each Memorial and Veterans' day:

* The fear of being 19 and in his first major battle, chasing the Germans back into their homeland.

* The confusing feelings of teaming with a fellow American to shoot at a young German soldier, seeing him drop and die, and then finding photos of the soldier's girlfriend among his belongings.

"Was he a poor soldier like me?" Gilbert wrote decades later in his memoirs. "It really got to me. I can see him and his young face in my mind. ... Anyway, we went on."

* The physical pain of metal tearing into his leg, surviving only because a much taller, broader soldier took the brunt of the explosion near the famed Remagen Bridge in Germany.

* The sadness of knowing that soldier – who, in essence, shielded him from death – didn't live to see his family again. The sadness of learning that on the final day of the war, a good friend was killed. The sadness of seeing the concentration camp at Dachau, where the smell of death permeated his senses forever.

* The disgust of watching in person the pompous, arrogant Nazis -- men who while serving as Adolf Hitler's brain trust orchestrated and perpetrated the Holocaust -- smirk and scoff at the court no differently than did former Iraqi dictator Saddam Hussein during his war crimes trial six year ago.

* And, finally, the joy of coming home in one piece in January 1946.

There were so many just like him, young men called to do their duty, to punish the murderers and aggressors of the world and to defend freedom. Until the winter of 1944 and spring of 1945, though, Gilbert thought a battle meant beating Turlock High in basketball, or teaming with Lee Brooks to go undefeated in doubles and win the Section tennis title.

That soon changed. He graduated from **Modesto** High in June 1944 and received his draft notice a month later. He tried to enlist in the Navy, which rejected him because he is color blind. The Army didn't discriminate and took him. Suspecting he might not survive the war, Gilbert told his longtime girlfriend, Ginny, that she was free to date other men while he was gone.

He went to Fort Hood, Texas, only to have the usual 16 weeks of basic training lopped to 12 because of the heavy losses endured during the Battle of the Bulge. The military needed replacements ASAP and he soon found himself crossing the Atlantic on the famed Queen Elizabeth liner. By winter, he trudged through the snow while pushing the Germans back into their homeland.

After he was wounded March 10, 1945, he went to a hospital in France, recuperating there when the war in Europe ended two months later.

He figured he'd be heading home soon. He guessed wrong, because he soon found himself standing smack-dab in the middle of perhaps the most important event of the immediate post-war era.

The Army sent him to **Nuremberg**, Germany, where the trials of the 21 worst-of-the-worst Nazis were about to begin. And on the first day, Nov. 20, 1945, Gilbert drew an assignment he'll never forget.

Thanks to a teacher at **Modesto** High who used the war news as a teaching tool, Gilbert was well aware of Hermann Goering, Rudolph Hess, Albert Jodl, Julius Streicher and others on trial for crimes against humanity.

When he got to **Nuremberg**, these monsters of the Third Reich were right there in front of him and, one day, alongside him. He escorted Goering, who helped build the Nazi war machine leading up to the war, founded the Gestapo and at one time was considered Hitler's hand-picked successor, from his cell into the courtroom.

"I'm standing next to Hermann Goering, and he's so short," Gilbert said. "I couldn't believe it. Short and fat. I was expecting something else. We walked them to the courtroom, led them to their places and then stood behind the two rows of defendants."

In one widely used photograph from the trial, Gilbert can be seen standing in the back row, second from the left.

"That's me," he said.

When he wasn't inside the courtroom, he sometimes spent his off-duty time in the listening area to hear some of the testimony.

"I was infatuated with the trial," he said.

The Army rotated soldiers through several duties, never allowing them to speak to the Germans, who wouldn't have spoken to them anyway.

"They thought we were way below them," Gilbert said. "They thought they were better than us."

On some days, he spent 90-minute shifts standing at the door of one of the cells, watching the prisoner's every move, ready to move in and stop them from committing suicide before they could be convicted and hanged.

"We watched them eat, get dressed, pee ... you name it," Gilbert said.

He took a particular disliking to Streicher, a onetime newspaper publisher on trial because he spent decades inciting hatred against the Jews.

"He was a horrible man," Gilbert said. "Just horrible."

Gilbert left before the trial was over, coming home on an emergency leave in January 1946 because his mother fell and broke her hip. He mustered out two months later and set upon wooing the love of his life -- Ginny -- whom he'd told to see other men as he went off to war. She did, but only because she thought he wanted to end their relationship.

"I had to win her back," he said.

And did. They've been married ever since. He turned 86 last week, and they now live in Angels Camp. A couple of strokes have slowed him, but the memories remain.

Goering, the Nazi general Gilbert escorted at the trial, committed suicide by swallowing cyanide in his cell just two hours before his scheduled execution in October 1946.

"How could that have been?" Gilbert wonders today. "They watched his cell all of the time."

War, he'll tell you, is about death. He stood 67 years ago in the courtroom with men who orchestrated so much of it and brought great heartache to the world -- heartache revisited every Memorial Day.

"It was an experience I'll never forget," Gilbert said.

Robert Gilbert died in Chula Vista, CA., in 2017.

Jeff Jardine / The Modesto Bee

Charles Fenley, left, with Bob Thompson.

D-Day book cements 5-decade friendship across north Modesto street

June 6, 2017

   During their 50-plus years as neighbors in north Modesto, Bob Thompson developed an undying respect for Charles Fenley, who lives directly across the street.

"I was never a fan of Tom Brokaw," Thompson, a retired high school history teacher, told me. "But when he wrote 'The Greatest Generation,' I became a fan. As I look around Modesto for the greatest generation, he's right there."

He nodded toward Fenley, sitting in an easy chair a few feet away. But the book that really cemented their friendship wasn't Brokaw's 1998 bestseller. It was one Thompson bought from the United States Naval Institute four years earlier, titled "Assault on Normandy: First-Person Accounts From the Sea Services."

"I was looking for something to give Charlie," Thompson said. "He'd done some electrical work for me and wouldn't take anything for it. So I bought him the book and brought it over to him."

Courtesy of Charles Fenley

Charles Fenley, center.

A few minutes later, Fenley came running across the street to Thompson's house, all excited.

"There's a picture of my boat in there!" Fenley said, showing Thompson the photo of Landing Craft Tank 528, his second boat at Normandy after his original, LCT 522, suffered hull damage.

"Then, about 15 minutes later, he came over again," Thompson said. "He said, 'There's a picture of me and the crew in the book!' "

What are the chances of that? But then, what were the chances of Fenley's boat landing on Utah Beach on the morning of June 6, 1944 – D-Day – to find minimal German resistance when the battles raged along the Normandy coast and claimed 2,499 American lives among the 4,413 Allied deaths, the majority at Omaha Beach?

A native of Stockton, Fenley once delivered the Stockton Record newspaper, loved to sing and was known around Stockton as "The Singing Paperboy." He went to high school only for a year before quitting to work in construction. After the U.S. entered World War II both in the Pacific and

Europe, he enlisted in the Navy in 1942 as an 18-year-old. He trained as a gunner and electrician. They sent him from New York to Plymouth, England aboard the Queen Mary in 1943, where he joined the LCTs.

Bad weather pushed the D-Day invasion back a day, and when it began his LCT was among those assigned to land at Utah Beach. The Allied forces pounded the German defenses. The Americans lost 197 men out of the 21,000 soldiers who stormed Utah Beach. Fenley's LCT 522 didn't get ashore until after 10:30 a.m.

"By the time we hit the beach, we owned it," Fenley said. "We caught no German fire. We really lucked out. I stayed on that beach for almost a year." The LCTs absolutely were vital to the war effort. At Normandy, they shuttled soldiers, supplies and ammo across the English Channel to France, and then carried wounded Americans back to England on the return trips.

"One day on the beach, I ran into an MP (military policeman) from Stockton," Fenley said. "We're talking, and all of a sudden he jumps to attention. There was a general standing in a Jeep, and he wore a pearl-handled pistol. It was General Patton."

Shortly after Germany surrendered in May 1945, he found himself on a transport ship headed back to New York and, eventually, to Stockton. There, he met and married Annabelle Fassat in 1946.

"She put up with me for 70 years," Fenley said. She died a year ago. During that time, he went on to start the 5-Minute Car Wash chain that included three car washes in Modesto and a fourth in Bakersfield. He often hired employees with disabilities, and later giving those with prison records a chance to restart their lives on the outside.

His son, Michael, now runs the business. Charles' eyes are no longer as sharp as his mind, and neighbor Thompson comes over to visit with him daily often to read aloud, a chapter a day, to his 92-year-old friend.

"It's been a privilege to live across the street from this guy for the last 51, 52 years," Thompson said. "I'm so grateful for what he did during the war years. The whole war depended on the LCTs."

Which is why, in 1994, Thompson bought the book and gave it to Fenley only to find out Fenley actually is in it.

"I hadn't read the book before I gave it to him," Thompson said. "It gave me great pleasure and it brought me to tears."

A chapter a day, indeed. And the book he is reading to Fenley now?

"Assault on Normandy: First-Person Accounts From the Sea Services."
So timely, so fitting.

Joan Barnett Lee / The Modesto Bee

Les Williams, a member of the famed Tuskegee Airmen, at home in Patterson.

A Tuskegee Airman lands in Patterson

February 8, 2015

February is Black History Month. It's a time earmarked for emphasizing and educating about the tragedies and triumphs, the prejudices and the fight for equality that continues today.

It's a history that began in this country with slavery, and now focuses on the lives of Dr. Martin Luther King Jr., Rosa Parks, Jackie Robinson, President Barack Obama and others who sought to break down the racial barriers.

Sometimes, though, people need only to get to know their neighbors to meet someone who can testify to the injustices that African Americans have endured.

Les Williams lives with his wife and daughter in a two-story home in a decade-old housing development in Patterson. It's been a tough transition for the 95-year-old, moving a year ago from the more familiar surroundings of San Mateo, where he spent most of his life, to the quiet, small town on the county's West Side.

Few, if any, of his neighbors know Williams served during World War II as a member of the famed Tuskegee Airmen, the first black aviators in American military history. Williams, in fact, rose to the rank of captain.

Joan Barnett Lee / The Modesto Bee
Les Williams' medal.

Nor would they know that he was an accomplished tap dancer who ran a dance studio in San Mateo for 30 years or that he graduated from Stanford Law and became an attorney at age 50. Or that his cousin Archie Williams won the 400-meter run in the 1936 Olympic Games in Berlin, the same in which black American athletes led by Jesse Owens, who won four golds, left German dictator Adolf Hitler in a snit and refusing to shake their hands.

Or that Les Williams spent summers of his youth visiting relatives in Southern California, where he became friends with Robinson, later competing against him when Williams attended the College of San Mateo and Robinson starred at Pasadena City College well before going on to break major league baseball's color barrier in 1947.

A remarkable life, indeed, and one in which Williams simply refused to take "no" – specifically, "No, because you are black" – for an answer.

After the attack on Pearl Harbor, Williams knew he would be drafted into the Army. Hearing the Army Air Corps had begun training black pilots, he weighed the risks of flying against those of serving in the infantry, having seen others return from the war with permanent wounds. His future as a performer after the war hinged on surviving it intact.

"I didn't want to lose my ability to dance," Williams said. "I'd rather crash and die. Better than losing limbs."

The Tuskegee Airmen – so named because many pilots already had been in the Civil Pilot Training Program at Tuskegee University in Alabama –

were under the command of white officers, virtually all of whom remained steeped in the racism against blacks, using the N-word at every turn, Williams said.

"It was disgusting," he said. "Prejudice is a nasty thing – a terrible thing."

He passed his solo flight even though the officer who tested him flunked most other black pilots. Williams was confident to the point of being cocky, a smart and a natural leader. He was promoted to sergeant and ultimately to captain. But rank didn't matter. Skin color did.

It irked him that black officers were being trained by white officers who had less flying time, and that the white officers had a club with a fully stocked bar at Freeman Field base in Indiana. In fact, black officers also were prohibited from using the post exchange and theater, the latter of which was open to German POWs held at the base. Yes, German prisoners of war.

"The white pilots would not let us use their nightclub," Williams said. "When you get tired, a little drink wouldn't hurt. Helps you relax. But they prohibited black fliers from coming in. We just wanted a little merriment. We decided to bring it to a conflict."

In what became known as the Freeman Field Mutiny in the spring of 1945, black officers went in groups of three and tried to get into the club. They were denied drinks. One of them, Lt. Roger Terry, brushed up against a white major, who proceeded to file charges against Terry and two others.

So 300 black officers decided to protest, with about 100 of them marching to the officers club only to find it closed. The next day, 50 single officers and 50 married officers were randomly arrested for their actions. Williams wasn't one of them, even though he participated.

Terry, however, wasn't so fortunate. While acquitted of disobeying an order, he was convicted of "jostling" the white officer, fined $150, busted down in rank and dishonorably discharged. In 1995, Terry received a full pardon, had his rank restored and the $150 fine refunded.

While the Tuskegee Airmen fighter pilots saw extensive duty and performed extremely well, the B-25s that Williams and his fellow airmen flew didn't see combat. The war ended before they could get into it. Part of him felt relieved. The other half?

"It bothered me," he said. "We were right at the brink."

He left the service after the war and tried to find work as a commercial airline pilot.

"One of them (airline executives) told him to pick up the broom in the corner," his daughter Penny Williams said. "That that was the only job he'd ever get in aviation."

Consequently, he moved on in life, attending Stanford for his undergraduate degree while starting up his dance studio. For years, he rarely spoke about his experiences as a Tuskegee Airman.

"People didn't believe he was a pilot, so he stopped talking about it," said daughter Penny, who in 2010 co-wrote with him a book titled "Victory: Tales of a Tuskegee Airman" (available on Amazon.com).

Eventually, others did talk about it. Williams and other surviving Tuskegee Airmen received the Congressional Gold Medal from President George W. Bush in 2007. And Williams attended Obama's first inauguration two years later.

Among Williams' dance students in San Mateo was a young boy named Lynn Swann, who went on to become a star receiver at USC, win four Super Bowls with the NFL's Pittsburgh Steelers and now is a Pro Football Hall of Famer.

When San Mateo's Serra High inducted Swann into its hall of fame in 2012, he used his time to honor Williams, who attended the ceremony.

"Les Williams is the true hometown hero here today," Swann told the crowd that day.

The Williams family, including Elsie – his wife of 70 years – and daughters Paula and Penny, all moved to Stanislaus County's West Side last year. It's been a difficult adjustment well into his 90s, with new surroundings and none of his old friends around.

Indeed, Patterson has a relatively new neighbor, and one whose story is why black history is such an important part of American history and needs to be told.

Les Williams died at 95 in 2015.

Soldiers have to beg for supplies

September 12, 2004

In mid-August, just days before they shipped out to Texas for training, members of a California National Guard unit summoned a welder to the armory in Oakdale.

They had scrounged up slabs of quarter-inch-thick metal needed to fortify the Humvees they'll drive when they eventually get to Iraq, as they expect. But the pieces were too long for the container available for transport, so Eric Ender, who works for Taylor & Sons Welding and Machine in Oakdale, went over to make them fit.

"They were taking the stuff to (add the armor) themselves once they got over there," Ender said. "I just cut them in half."

Ender finished the job in an hour or so. The charges came to about $70. He said when he told them the amount, Guard members began reaching into their pockets, pooling their cash to pay the bill.

"I got the impression they were taking up a collection," Ender said.

Ender wasn't about to charge the soldiers. He waived the fee and returned to the shop.

"I was a little flabbergasted," he said. "It's kind of amazing. We spend $400 billion a year on defense and these guys were going to pay for their own armor? I asked one guy if they had to buy their own sleeping bags and food, too."

Passing the hat to pay the umpire of a Little League game is one thing. But you'd like to think soldiers going to war wouldn't have to pony up to thicken the skins of their Humvees.

"Only 20 percent of the Humvees are armored," Ender said the guardsmen told him. "And they're shooting at 100 percent of our (soldiers) over there."

We've heard all kinds of stories about soldiers in Iraq enduring supply shortages.

In The Bee's Letters to the Editor Aug. 25, Marine Lance Cpl. Jonathan C. Schenk of Modesto pleaded for donations of equipment the military isn't providing. Soldiers, he wrote, need the kinds of items that make "our job a lot easier."

His wish list ranged from AA batteries and Sharpie permanent markers to tactical combat goggles, raised butt-stock pads for M-16 rifles and a bunch of other things specific to soldiering in the desert.

And CBS last week aired interviews with parents who have lost children in the war. Some said they still are sending much-needed supplies to those who served alongside their sons or daughters.

During World War II, Americans sacrificed at home. They rationed meat, tires and gas. They grew vegetables in victory gardens so as not to diminish the food supply for troops overseas. By the time the war ended, the nation's support system and industrial machine became so effective that when my grandfather steamed back from the South Pacific, he watched perfectly good Jeeps and heavy equipment being dumped into the ocean.

The military didn't need them. So they were thrown away.

The same thing happened, Oakdale's Mike Reiff said, when he returned from Vietnam. He said Jeeps and helicopters -- some without so much as a scratch in the paint -- were shoved overboard rather than be hauled home and sold for public use.

But in the ongoing quagmire known as the Iraq war, equipment shortages are common and should embarrass the government.

The Pentagon is questioning why Halliburton, the government's supply contractor in Iraq, can't account for $1.8 billion -- a figure generated from roughly 43 percent of the bills audited so far, Reuters reported. Think of how much armor $1.8 billion would buy for the Humvees -- installed.

Think of how many combat goggles it would provide. If Schenk believes they will help him do his job better and stay alive, then he deserves them. The costs of war are great enough, with more than 1,000 American soldiers now dead.

Young men and women join the military knowing they might have to pay a price at the end.

They shouldn't have to pay up front, too.

Courtesy of The Modesto Bee
Mike Stavrakakis, left, pictured with Melvin Crank, began delivering books, magazines and other items to Veterans Affairs clinics throughout Northern California.

Ex-Navy man fills veterans' need to read

November 11, 2008

In 1961, as tensions between the Soviet Union and United States built toward what would become the Cuban missile crisis, the Navy recalled Korean War veteran Mike Stavrakakis of Modesto to active duty.

(Oh, and don't forget your sunglasses and the Coppertone, Mike. We're sending you to witness thermonuclear test explosions at Christmas Island in the Indian Ocean.)

After leaving the Navy again a year later, he visited the veterans' hospital in Livermore to be checked for radiation exposure.

"I'd glow in the dark," joked Stavrakakis, who worked for Pacific Bell for 37 years after leaving the Navy.

He arrived at the hospital about two hours early one day for his scheduled appointment, so he went to the hospital's library to read. Just one problem:

"There were no books," said Stavrakakis, 80. "The cupboard was bare."

He asked officials there if they would accept books and magazines. Yes, they told him, with two conditions:

"No sex books and no cookbooks," he said, setting up the punchline. "(The veteran patients are) too old for sex and they can't cook."

A few weeks later, he delivered a couple of boxes of reading materials. Then he collected some more and took them to the veterans' facilities at Palo Alto and Yountville.

He did same when the veterans medical clinic opened on McHenry Avenue in 2001 and again when the new veterans center opened on Carpenter Road in July.

He makes a book drop at each of those places every other month or so, and estimates he's gathered and distributed more than 3,000 books since he began 46 years ago.

In fact, on this Veterans Day you could say Stavrakakis has never stopped serving his country. He serves his fellow veterans, making their lives a bit more pleasant at the hospitals and clinics. He and fellow Navy and Korean War veteran Melvin "Bud" Crank snag books wherever they can find them: garage and yard sales, moving sales, church groups and simply by asking.

Once, he went to a house where a woman's wares included both books and plants. She'd priced a box at $5. He asked her to donate it to the veterans and she refused.

"But there was a guy who was buying $50 worth of plants and told her she had to give me the box of books or the deal was off," Stavrakakis said.

"She hesitated, but she gave me the books."

When the new veterans center opened last summer, Stavrakakis asked center director Steve Lawson where he'd find the library.

"There was no place to put one, and they didn't have any books," Stavrakakis said. "So Melvin and I went begging, borrowing and stealing."

They went to Warden's outlet office furnishings store and "put the bite" on sales manager Sean Keon.

"He took us in the back and showed me what he had," Stavrakakis said. "Three identical bookcases."

When Keon learned they wanted the shelves for the Veterans Center, he donated them.

"Within a half hour, we had a full-blown library going," Stavrakakis said, promising to expand it in the near future.

His trips to Livermore, Palo Alto and Yountville bring him nothing beyond personal satisfaction.

"People ask me how much money I get for selling the books up there," he said. "Heck, it costs me $50 just for gas to go over there and back. It's a labor of love. I'm just glad I'm in good health and can do it."

He sometimes delivers people as well as books.

"Whenever I have an appointment in Livermore or Palo Alto, he takes me over there," Crank said.

"I haul 'em up and back," Stavrakakis said. "Sometimes I bring back more than I came with."

That's because some vets will ride the bus over, finish their appointments and not want to wait several hours before the bus returns to the valley.

"I'll say, 'Anyone going back to Modesto?' " he said.

Each morning, he and several other veterans gather for coffee and conversation at the McDonald's on McHenry Avenue. They've been doing this for about 15 years. Their group once had about a dozen vets, mostly from World War II and the Korean War.

"You start the day off with a laugh and it makes all the difference in the world," Crank said.

"Lots of people don't understand us," Stavrakakis said. "But if a guy doesn't show, we call to see if he's still alive. We've lost some guys over the past few years."

Those who do show know he'll probably have a favor to ask, and it invariably involves helping other veterans.

"He'll volunteer you to death," Crank said. "But if you have him for a friend, you can't have a better friend in the world. He'd do anything for you."

Yes, he's still serving his country -- by serving others who served their country, 46 years later.

And when he talks about it, he just glows.

At the time this went to print, Stavrakakis said he's delivered over 67,000 items to Veterans clinics throughout Northern California, with more on the way

.

Cold War still felt by Turlock veteran

August 17, 2011

One evening half a century ago today, Pieter Hoex and an Army buddy partied hard in the enlisted men's club at a base in West Germany.

The buddy, Hoex said, partied harder.

"He needed two men to hold him up," said Hoex, a 71-year-old Turlock resident. So when the base alarm system summoned the troops, Hoex had to recruit some help to get his friend back into fighting shape.

"We gave him a cold shower," Hoex said. "It didn't help. Then we got him dressed in battle gear for the assembly."

Courtesy of The Modesto Bee

Peter Hoex and wife Marianne.

A few words from their commanding officer did the trick, though.

"Colonel Glover (Johns Jr.) said, 'Men, we're going to Berlin.' From that time on, my buddy was stone sober. That shook him up."

Same for all 1,500 soldiers in the U.S. Army's 1st Battle Group, 18th Infantry, 8th Infantry Division — Hoex included — as the Cold War heated up in Europe. Five days earlier, the Soviets began building the Berlin Wall, which quickly came to represent the line dividing freedom and oppression. The wall's 50th anniversary Saturday drew minimal media attention, in no small part because the wall came down in 1989. But if you were alive in the 1950s or '60s and even into the 1970s, the Cold War seemed far more ominous to Americans at home than did the Korean or Vietnam wars fought abroad.

Bolstered by the threat of nuclear attacks and huge arsenals on both sides, tensions with the Soviets changed the way we lived. We were schooled on where to go in the event of a nuclear attack, what food supplies to keep on hand and more.

I suspect few kids today have ever heard the term "fallout shelter" or even "civil defense." Yet that underlying fear remained part of the fabric of society for more than two decades in this country.

When World War II ended, the victorious Allies split defeated Germany into two nations, East and West. The United States, Britain and France rebuilt West Germany. East Germany became nothing more than a Soviet satellite nation. Likewise, Berlin, in East Germany, got rezoned: The Americans, British and French on one side and the Soviets on the other. West Berlin was an island surrounded by socialism, and the Soviets tried to starve the West Berliners by cutting off access to the city. The United States responded with the Berlin Airlift, flying 270,000 planes carrying supplies in 1948 and 1949, until the Soviets lifted the blockade.

In 1961, the Soviets began building the Berlin Wall and made a great show of military force. So President John F. Kennedy ordered U.S. troops into West Berlin.

The agreement with the Soviets allowed the U.S. military to pass through East Germany to West Berlin on the Autobahn, Hoex remembers. He and his infantry comrades were part of a convoy that included 260 2½-ton trucks — called "deuce-and- a-half's" — loaded with soldiers and supplies.
They motored roughly 110 miles through East Germany, passing Soviet tanks stationed about a mile apart, with machine-gun nests and snipers in between. It was intimidating, Hoex said — more so for some of the older war-tested veterans than younger guys who didn't know any better.

"We had four NCOs (noncommissioned officers), and all had been in Korea," Hoex said. "One was sweating it more than the others, but they all were sweating."

Because if even one Soviet soldier suddenly broke ranks and fired on the U.S. troops.

"We'd have been sitting ducks," Hoex said. "Someone made the decision to put all of our ammo in the bottom of the trailer and our duffel bags on top."

Hoex might have taken a bullet for a nation not yet his own, and all because he wanted to track down an old flame in Holland.

He was born in 1940 in the Dutch East Indies (Indonesia) and was a toddler when the Japanese gained control and imprisoned his family in a concentration camp. He recalls that when his brother died, the Japanese soldiers forced his mother to dig the child's grave during a heavy rainstorm.

British forces liberated the Dutch when the war ended, fighting Indonesians who opposed the resumption of Dutch rule. But many remained in the camp for a few months because the first caravan out, carrying women and children, was attacked by the Indonesians.
"They were slaughtered," Hoex said.

His family returned to Europe in 1949. He came to the United States in 1960 and, a year later, joined the Army as a noncitizen.
"I wanted to get back to Europe," Hoex said. "I had a girlfriend there at the time."

He got back to Europe, all right, but they never connected. Stationed near Mannheim in West Germany, his trip to West Berlin lasted four months. "Driving into Berlin, there were thousands cheering us," he said. "We got a hero's welcome. They treated us royally."

When he returned to his base in the winter, he attended a dance and saw a young woman sitting with her mother. He asked the girl to dance. She declined. So he asked her mother, who accepted. Eventually, the daughter came around.

So much for the old girlfriend he'd taken the European assignment to find. Hoex found his future wife, Marianne, that night. He mustered out of the Army in September 1963, returned to the States and began working on securing her a visa to come to the United States. They were married in Las Vegas in December of that year.

They later worked for the Milpitas Unified School District, near San Jose — she for 23 years, he for 18 -- before retiring and moving to Turlock in 2003.

Now, 50 years after his trip into Berlin, only sections of the wall remain as tourist attractions. Germany is one nation again and the Soviet Union dissolved.

The threat of the Cold War that existed then is now a footnote in history, supplanted by the Sept. 11 attacks and wars in Afghanistan and Iraq. Only Hoex and the others who rode through East Germany in August 1961 understand how close they came to total calamity.

"If any of the Russians or East Germans had a trigger finger," he said, "they could have started World War III."

On war's threshold

November 11, 2007

On this Veterans Day, meet a man who likes to say he was a "guest of the Gestapo" in a Nazi prisoner of war camp during World War II, but refuses to consider himself a prisoner.

"All they had was my body," Merced's Peter Komlenich said. "My mind was home with my daughter and bride."

Komlenich has another distinction, too. He's the man who nearly started World War III.

"That would have been me," said Komlenich, who controlled four nuclear bombs in the belly of a B-52 during one Cold War mission.

As the generation of U.S. World War II veterans dwindles by 1,000 to 1,500 a day, according to various news agencies, there's been a frantic effort to chronicle the memories of those who served and fought. But then there's a guy like Komlenich, who spent 30 years in the military -- in the war and afterward -- and whose career had some equally important moments. None was more important than the day when he was perhaps an hour or so away from obliterating the Kremlin and all that surrounded it.

In October 1962, Komlenich served as a radarman/bombardier on a B-52 with the Strategic Air Command at Castle Air Force Base in Atwater. The Pentagon had determined that the Soviet Union had been supplying Cuba with nuclear weapons, which the Soviets denied even as their supply ships were headed to the island nation 90 miles south of Florida.

President Kennedy confronted Soviet Premier Nikita Khrushchev, and the Cuban missile crisis went from a simmer to a full boil. Kennedy demanded the Soviets turn their ships around before they reached a designated point on the map. If they didn't, Kennedy promised, the United States would attack the Soviet Union.

The Soviets ultimately caved, calling back their ships. What they probably didn't know is just how close they came to being attacked, Komlenich said.

"That was something," he said. "You never hear about this. Few people ever knew about it."

A day earlier, Komlenich and the rest of the B-52 crew bade goodbye to their families at Castle, their stomachs knotted from knowing their loved ones were at risk, too. Their mission was top secret. Komlenich could only act as if he were going on a normal training exercise, even though he knew that if the United States attacked, the Soviets would retaliate by hitting key military installations such as Castle.

The B-52 flew east overnight, refueling in midair just beyond the Atlantic coast and again over Greenland. The American plane, one of several involved in the mission, carried four Mark-VI nuclear weapons in its bomb bay, Komlenich said.

Their first of four targets would be the Kremlin, and they had reached the prescribed place where, if the Soviet ships didn't turn back, they would proceed with the bombing run that would trigger nuclear warfare.

Komlenich had studied maps and photos of the Kremlin, and he would have been the one to release the bombs that would have devastated the Soviet government complex and everything else within miles.

It was Oct. 28, 1962. The plane was in the air, waiting for the order to attack. Suddenly, the mission was aborted.

" ... I heard a shout from upstairs that the Soviet leader had 'blinked first,' and Russian ships had turned back and we had received the 'Green Dot' message and could head for home," Komlenich wrote in his memoirs. "When I got back with my family, I gave each one of them an extra hug and thanked the Lord for a safe mission."

Armageddon would have to wait for another day, and on someone else's watch.

Throughout his 94 years, Komlenich developed a penchant for coming home safe, if not always sound.

The Chicago native rode the rails as a hobo for two years as a teen during the Great Depression. He worked along the way for a home-cooked meal, but never for money.

Then, using a false birthday, he enlisted in the Army's Horse Cavalry in the 1930s. But he left rather than face a possible court-martial for giving the phony birth date. He joined the Civilian Conservation Corps, working on projects in the Ozarks of Arkansas and Missouri.

He returned to the hobo life briefly and then worked for International Harvester until 1941, when the Japanese bombed Pearl Harbor.

Komlenich wanted to fly fighter planes. But by then he was 28, two years too old to enlist as a pilot. So he used the birth certificate of his younger brother, Louis Komnenich, to sign up. Louis was a Marine paratrooper missing in action somewhere in the Pacific.

The translation of his family name from their native Montenegrin language on a birth certificate confused authorities, but allowed him to use his own name with his brother's birthday to get in, he said. The translation also explains why they spell their last names differently (Komlenich and Komnenich). In Montenegrin, the "l" and the "n" look and sound similar. It explains why current state voting records list Komlenich as 91, when in fact he is 94.

"I was born July 3, 1913," Komlenich said.

He went to flight school but shattered both ear drums in training. After surgery, he was assigned to bombardier school.

"It turned out to be a blessing," he said.

As a bombardier instead of pilot or gunner, he was in the middle of a B-24 Liberator during a bombing run, when a swarm of German ME-109s shot down his plane over Italy.

"One guy, a substitute gunner, got killed in the turret," Komlenich said. "A life for a (trigger) finger."

Because it failed, Komlenich likes to say he flew only 12½ missions. He was taken to an interrogation center, then to Stalag Luft I, a prisoner of war camp in Barth, Germany, primarily for aviation officers. One day, near Easter 1944, a German camp guard struck Komlenich as he stood near the fence chatting with some Russian women just outside. He defended himself and was hauled away for questioning.

He realized he still had, in his jacket, a piece of silk that bore a map of escape tunnels being dug. If they had caught him with it, he likely would have been executed and endangered his barracks mates as well. He claimed he needed to use the restroom, and it flushed down the toilet on his second try.

Soon, though, Komlenich stood before a jury that certainly didn't consist of his peers. His trial for assaulting the prison guard was on.

"I was the only American in the room," Komlenich recalled.

The proceedings in this kangaroo court might have been downright comical had his life not been at stake. For there stood the strapping 200-pound German prison guard whining to a six-man, all-German jury that this emaciated 105-pound Yank prisoner of war had somehow violently assaulted him.

Then came the preordained verdict:

"In accordance with the Geneva Convention during time of war, you have been found guilty of striking a prison official. You will be executed by a firing squad as soon as arrangements can be made."

Some ranking American officers explained to the commandant why Komlenich should get a new trial.

" ... Colonel Spicer, Colonel Zemke and Group Captain Weir visited the German Camp Kammandant Colonel Warnsredt and told him that if anything happened to me he would be hung," Komlenich wrote in his memoirs. "Fortunately, the Allies were winning the war on all fronts during the Spring of 1944 or I wouldn't be alive to tell about this event."

This time, he got 30 days in the "cooler," a frigid form of confinement in German POW camps, and a diet consisting of bread and water every other day. But he lived to walk out of there when the Allied forces closed in, the Germans fled and the POWs took over the camp in April 1945.

Komlenich decided to stay in the military after the war and was assigned to the SAC. He flew in the B-36 program and then in the B-52s at Castle. He spends much of his time these days at the Castle Air Museum educating visitors about the war machines and the men who flew them.

Two years ago, he finally returned the birth certificate he had "borrowed" from his brother in 1941.

Although Peter Komlenich loves to tell his stories about being shot down and becoming a "guest of the Gestapo," perhaps the more important mission of his life was the other one he didn't complete: The one in October 1962, that ended before he could start World War III.

Pete Komlenich died at 101 in 2014.

Changing of the guard

Vets who served in Korea, Vietnam take lead in parade

November 12, 2009

Earl Wood spent the final months of World War II on Okinawa, preparing to invade Japan.

"Then they dropped the bomb, and we didn't have to go in," the 86-year-old Modestan said.

Wednesday, he watched from the sidewalk as the Veterans Day procession went past him -- physically and symbolically – up I Street and then down 14th to Graceada Park. Past him, because with this parade the Veterans Day torch officially passed from the World War II generation to those who fought in Korea and Vietnam.

A few World War II veterans marched. Others, most in their mid-80s, stepped to the sidelines as age and declining health has turned them from participants into spectators.

"There's so few of us left," Wood said, elated that the parade has been re-energized -- by desire and by necessity -- by the next generation. "If they don't do it, it goes away."

The good news is that the parade isn't going anywhere except up I Street and over to Graceada Park again next year, the year after and so on. The Korea and Vietnam vets will see to that, with the Desert Storm, Iraq and Afghanistan war vets after them.

"It was breaking new ground for us," said Steve Lawson, director of the Modesto Vet Center, which was instrumental in staging the parade. A Vietnam veteran, Lawson served as the grand marshal. The center has served more than 600 veterans, from World War II to Iraq and Afghanistan, providing counseling for veterans suffering from post-traumatic stress disorder.

The vast majority of the center's clients, though, are Vietnam vets. Some returned from Southeast Asia only to be scorned by an American public that had turned against the war and took its collective frustration out on those who fought it. They endured insults. And virtually all of them struggled to re-adjust to civilian life in a country so different from the one they left.

Wednesday, they finally could bask in the appreciation of a public that either no longer blames them for the war or is simply too young to remember it. Many of the Vietnam vets participated in a Veterans Day event for the very first time, some 34 years after the war ended.

The mood and the event were completely different than Veterans Day parades of the past. It once ended with a ceremony at a cemetery on Scenic Drive. Now it journeys to Graceada Park, where organizations set up information booths, followed by speeches and music in Mancini Bowl. Organizers succeeded in turning the event into a celebration of the living veterans rather than a duplication of Memorial Day, which so appropriately honors those killed in wartime. Most Americans, including many in the media, don't understand the distinction between the two.

In fact, the problem now would be apathy -- not antagonism. "My generation ... there's not enough patriotism," said Army vet Brian Stutzman, who survived 33 roadside bomb attacks while serving two tours of duty in Iraq.

The 34-year-old Hilmar resident joined the parade to remind others his age of the role the military plays in the nation's security. "My girls know what the colors of the flag mean," he said.

They are in the minority. On a day when the schools, banks and government offices closed in the veterans' honor, 1,000 to 1,500 people lining the streets meant others slept in, played video games or simply enjoyed a day off. So be it. That's yet another one of the rights these veterans fought to protect.

Those who stayed away missed a re-energized event that only promises to get better, and a chance to say "thank you" to a new generation of veterans who, in many cases, have really been there all along.

The World War II vets remain beloved and revered even as they dwindle in numbers. The stories of their heroics and experiences are priceless and still need to be told. But the responsibility to keep alive the Veterans Day parade now belongs to the next generation.

A number of World War II veterans, Wood among them, proudly saluted their successors from the sidewalks.

Earl Wood died in August 2017.

Despite fighting in wars apart, two vets find they're brothers in arms

July 30, 2011

Two weeks ago, when The Bee invited Vietnam War veterans to share their experiences in Southeast Asia, we knew we'd get some compelling responses and moving stories.

Courtesy of Ronn Cossey
Vietnam veteran and Silver Star recipient Ronn Cossey.

We have. None, though, may be more moving and compelling than this one:

Four years ago, Army vet Ronn Cossey of Turlock was invited to ride in the parade and speak at the annual Veterans Car Show at Pismo Beach. The event raises money to aid veterans.

There he met Zeb Lane of Ohio, who had served in the Marines' Lima Company in Iraq. Lane's unit lost 23 men — 14 in a single explosion — in 2005. Lane was among the 40 survivors wounded in the fighting around Haditha.

He had come to Pismo Beach to auction artwork to benefit the Lima Company Memorial to be built in Columbus.

These men, who fought in different wars in different decades, spent hours talking that weekend. They compared battle notes and what has happened to them since leaving the military. They became friends. They formed a bond.

In Lane, the 63-year-old Cossey saw a younger version of himself — a veteran who experienced the horrors of war and will deal with them for the rest of his life.

In Cossey, the 30-year-old Lane found someone who understands combat, fought the internal war that followed, and who can help him navigate the emotional no-man's land of post-traumatic stress disorder.

Iraq War veteran Zeb Lane.
Courtesy of Zeb Lane

War does horrible things to good people, and many simply cannot turn in their demons when they muster out and return to civilian life.

"One night, I had bad flashbacks of PTSD," Lane said. "I called Ronn. We talked for hours and hours."

Cossey wanted to help Lane. Lane wants to help those who fought in Iraq or Afghanistan.

So they began writing letters back and forth. Cossey would tell Lane a story about Vietnam, his time in a tank battalion and life in Southeast Asia. War stories.

Lane would write back, telling Cossey about dealing with insurgents, improvised explosive devices and life in the Persian Gulf. War stories.

This went on for months, letter after letter that became chapter after chapter.

Similar wars and stories

They discovered their wars were similar. Vietnam became the war Americans said they never wanted to repeat. Iraq became the war, these veterans concluded, that repeated it.

In both wars, distinguishing between ally and enemy posed problems. Cossey described the perils of jungle warfare and never knowing where the snipers hid; Lane matched it with depictions of going house to house in Iraqi towns and cities, building to building, searching out and snuffing out insurgents.

Both men lost more friends and comrades than they could bear.

War, they concluded, is universally awful.

They've compiled their letters into a book they've titled "NamRaq." Like the group of veterans in Stanislaus County writing a book about their Vietnam experiences, Cossey and Lane find writing therapeutic and traumatic. Therapeutic because it helps them sort out their issues. Traumatic because they have to relive those life-altering moments.

They hold back nothing. They tell of moments that affected them deeply and still do. There's no political correctness, no caving to revisionist histories.

They were there. They know what it was like.

Cossey is sick and tired of hearing that the United States lost the Vietnam War. President John F. Kennedy's edict, he said, was to stop the spread of communism in the Pacific Rim.

"We did that," Cossey said. "The only place that is communist now that wasn't when we got there is South Vietnam."

Survivor's guilt

In the first chapter, Cossey explains what so many survivors from so many wars have felt and carried with them the rest of their lives.

"I am successful to many, but feel guilty because I am alive, and they aren't," Cossey wrote. "I should have fought harder, to the death if need be, so my brothers would still be alive. Survivor's guilt they call it, and sometimes it controls my whole life, but I will keep fighting it with all the other horrors that I remember."

Lane wrote about his disgust with Vice President Dick Cheney's ties to Halliburton, the only company allowed to bid on providing services in Iraq, and how its subsidiary, KBR, fed the troops. Cheney, Halliburton's chief executive officer from 1995 to 2000, earned stock options and deferred CEO pay from Halliburton while serving as vice president in George W. Bush's administration.

"Granted, KBR provided good chow," Lane wrote. "But where is the incentive to end a war when your companies are making a fortune off of the war? That is all I am going to say about that topic."

Both men wrote of hitting the ground upon arriving in their war zones. When Cossey landed in South Vietnam in 1967, fighting greeted him at the airport.

"The heat hit me like a blast furnace!" Cossey wrote. "Then I noticed everyone was running to get off the plane, there were soldiers that hit the deck, even the flight crew. What the hell was that noise? It sounded like a hundred freight trains going through the air.

"Then the explosions, Machine gun fire, more explosions, burning buildings, people dead, dying and screaming. I never forgot those sounds of those people dying, and screaming, please someone help me, save me, save me, I'm hit, Where's mom?"

Lane's outfit came under mortar fire as its helicopters reached the Haditha Dam in Iraq.

Common bonds

Chapter matching chapter, story matching story.

Cossey wrote about engaging in combat 87 out of 91 days during the Tet Offensive of 1968.

Lane detailed the explosion that claimed 14 of his "brothers" in Iraq in 2005.

After Vietnam, Cossey worked in construction and fighting oil fires before going to work for Foster Farms. In 1999, he belatedly received a Silver Star for bravery, which he describes in the book.

Lane, a sergeant, is 100 percent disabled.
"I'm a liability," he said. "My medical condition is a liability."

He awaits his Purple Heart for the head injuries he suffered in Iraq. When bombs exploded close by, shrapnel shredded his wrist, and he fought through it all.

"I didn't try to get out of battle because of a frickin' scratch," he said. "(Members of his unit) look up to you as a leader. You get a major wound, you've got no choice. You keep going."

That is what these men are trying to do — keep going by helping each other knowing combat veterans everywhere will relate. They hope to find a publisher for their book, not so much to make money as to help other veterans. And if they do make money, they'll use it to help veterans.

Compelling stuff, indeed. Two men, two wars. Similar stories and parallel lives.

Ronn Cossey lives in Turlock. Zeb Lane lives in Ohio. Their book, "NamRaq: Letters That Heal" was published in 2014.

Jeff Jardine / The Modesto Bee
Vietnam veteran Phil Schmidt found that the war didn't end after he came home.

Modesto Vietnam veteran shares experience with 'moral injury'

November 5, 2014

Phil Schmitt spent two tours of duty in Vietnam loading 750-pound bombs into Air Force planes in bases at hellholes such as Da Nang and Phu Cat.

Most of the planes came back to be reloaded. The bombs, of course, didn't.

"I loaded thousands and thousands of tons of bombs," the 67-year-old Modesto resident said. "They went somewhere."

But it wasn't until the brass reassigned him to debrief the pilots after their bombing runs that he saw the real effects.

"Now I'm looking at films of the bombs exploding," Schmitt said. "Villages being hit. Seeing bodies on the ground. Children. The quality of those films was very good."

Collateral damage, long before anyone coined the term. Like so many others, he kept what he saw to himself, returning stateside when his hitch ended in 1970.

"Later, it comes into play," Schmitt said. "I turned to both heavy drinking and burying myself in my work. I didn't socialize. I was isolated. I didn't have many friends. I didn't relate well with people outside of the military."

Post-traumatic stress disorder? Sort of. It's generally the first diagnosis for any veteran with emotional issues. So, for decades, veterans such as Schmitt were treated for PTSD through Veterans Affairs and at places such as the Modesto Vet Center on Carpenter Road. But in recent years, it has become apparent to those treating PTSD that other forces churn inside these veterans – a condition only recently defined as moral injury.

PTSD stems from fear resulting from traumatic incidents. Moral injury shares some common symptoms, including anger, depression, anxiety and sleeping issues that can lead to drug or alcohol problems. But moral injury also involves sorrow, grief, guilt, shame and alienation, according to experts.

It affects some as it did Schmitt. They withdraw. They use alcohol or drugs to make their post-war world more palatable. Others, such as an Iraq War veteran from Ohio about whom I wrote because he co-wrote the book "NamRaq" with Turlock Vietnam vet Ronn Cossey, lose all concept of the consequences of their actions and behaviors back home. The Iraq vet experienced severe problems that resulted in stays in mental institutions, and he literally vanished into the Kentucky hills for a time, suspected (but later cleared) of committing crimes involving weapons.

Eventually, many, including Schmitt, reach out for help.

"I came here five or six times, but didn't come in," Schmitt said when we chatted Wednesday morning at the Vet Center on Carpenter Road. "My wife was upset with me. I had a stroke, but I went right back to drinking."

Finally, he walked through the doors. There he met Steve Lawson, the center's director, and Lance Stowe, its chaplain. They began treating him for PTSD.

"But PTSD therapy did not address the moral injury," Schmitt said. "It's an issue entirely on its own."

Once they understood what he'd been through, they began working to help him cope with it.

"It's been a lifesaver," Schmitt said. "I'm not sure where I would have ended up."

Stowe could help because, like Schmitt, he, too, bore responsibility for deaths that might have involved innocent civilians and possibly some friendly fire incidents.

"My moral injuries are managed, but they go back 40 years," Stowe said. Working with psychologists, he's come to understand the condition and why it is different than PTSD.

"They occupy two different spots in the brain," Stowe said. "The difference is that you can manage PTSD with medications or therapy. Moral injury doesn't turn off. It goes 24-7. Remorse, regret – the symptoms continue to play over and over in your mind."

PTSD, he said, can stem from a single event. Moral injury can be the result of multiple exposures. He spent 13 months in Vietnam. Schmitt did two tours of duty there. But many of today's military personnel will do several tours of duty. And, he said, they range from 18-year-old kids to 40-somethings in the National Guard reserves.

Stowe's artillery unit accounted for more than 350 confirmed casualties.

"I don't know what I'd have done if I'd had to return," he said. "We did lots of damage. Lots of things were the cost of war – the innocent loss of life – things that couldn't be prevented. I wasn't doing well when I came home. I went to college, but I was a mess."

Stowe said his spirituality has enabled him to deal with his issues and help others.

"I became a Christian when I came home after the war," he said. "I understand that forgiveness comes through Christ. Many of these guys don't really get that. But if there's an outside God who cares and loves them, they can forgive themselves."

He shares his story with those dealing with moral injury, explaining to them that what happened was an event and not the defining part of their lives, and that blame needs to be spread around – not borne solely by the individual. Some of the younger soldiers returning from Iraq and Afghanistan can't get past that, he said.

"They shot that little boy or old man," Stowe said. "Their prefrontal cortex (the part of the brain involved in abstract thinking, thought analysis and regulating behavior) is not fully developed. They go and do things and say, 'I can never forgive myself.'

"But when you employ body and soul, the spirit ... God never designed us to carry anger for long periods of time," he said.

Aligning with counseling efforts, superior courts throughout California – Stanislaus County included – are assessing whether so-called Veterans Courts would be beneficial. Rebecca Fleming, the county's courts administrator, she said she has met with veterans advocates including Stowe, government officials and others.

"We're trying to see what would be appropriate for this area," she said.

When a veteran commits a crime and the action can be linked to PTSD or moral injury issues, a Veterans Courts judge would determine the next step.

"Whether to commit them to therapy instead of throwing them into the court system," Stowe said.

Whatever works, he said. Stowe moderates a group session at the Vet Center every Tuesday from 10:30 a.m. to noon. Because the military has been more proactive in helping the Iraq and Afghanistan war vets reacclimate to civilian life, most of his members are Vietnam vets.

"Vietnam was worse because nothing was ever done about us," he said.

The help Schmitt receives gave him insight into what his father, H. Lawrence Schmitt, endured. An agent in the OSS, which preceded the CIA, Larry Schmitt was captured by the Germans in 1943 and tortured by the Gestapo until the war ended two years later.

"When he came home, he spent six months in the hospital," Schmitt said. "Talk about someone who suffered from PTSD. ... It took me well into my 60s to understand what went on with my dad."

That's because Schmitt kept torturing himself for things that happened in Vietnam. Not so much anymore.

"(Therapy) doesn't erase it," he said. "But I can deal with it better now."

Vietnam bullet scarred Modesto-area survivor, family

March 15, 2010

An act of bravery and leadership. An enemy bullet. A death that still resonates within two families on opposite sides of the country 42 years later.

Army Sgt. James L. Clark died in a firefight May 6, 1968, as his platoon tried to sever the North Vietnamese army's supply lines on the infamous Ho-Chi Minh Trail. Yet his family in LaGrange and Modesto knew only that he died. The Army gave them few details about his mission, his actions and the final moments of his life.

Clark's father, Gilbert, accepted his son's death with sort of a patriotic resignation. Gilbert died in the early 1970s. Clark's mother, Jacqueline, wrote numerous letters to military brass over the years before she died in 1994. Her daughter, Marti King of Modesto, continued searching for information but came up empty.

"It's a story of a how much a mother begged to know more about her son's passing," said Brian Gibson of Sellersville, Pa. "She went to her grave wanting to know more about Jim."

Gibson, Jim Clark's best friend in the Army, was there when it happened. He knew the details Clark's family yearned for. But from that day in 1968, and for the next 16 years, he buried the moment deep in the recesses of a soul he thought no longer existed. He contemplated suicide. He refused to talk about his Vietnam experiences with his counselor. He later learned he had a severe case of post-traumatic stress syndrome.

"I didn't care if I died," Gibson said. "I walked in a dead body for years."

Then one day, Gibson came across some letters he'd written to his grandparents in Delaware during the war, letters that detailed many of the things he'd seen and experienced in Vietnam. He'd written the last letter May 5, 1968, the day before Sgt. Jim Clark died.

"Two paper bags full of pictures and these letters came out," he said. "You recognize them immediately when they're in your handwriting."

He read them, and it hit him as he drove along a Pennsylvania interstate.

"It was like, 'Oh, my God. This connects me.' Things came back to me," he said. "There's something here I can't deny, and it's been a part of my life ever since then. There's a family out there and it was part of their lives, too."

Gibson decided to find Jim Clark's family and to tell them how their beloved son and brother died, how much he was respected by his unit, and to allow them to make some sense of his death.

It took some time to locate them. He finally did so in 2002 with help from the Internet. By then, the Virtual Wall Web site listed those killed during the war. He left a comment asking how to reach Clark's family. A woman who had been one of Clark's schoolmates responded. The woman called Marti King and told them a man wanted to meet with Clark's family.

"I was scared to death," he said. "I didn't want to be a ghost walking into their lives."

King was hesitant at first. Did this man really know her brother?

"She wanted to validate me," Gibson said. "(Clark) had a silver tooth in his smile. As soon as I mentioned that, she knew I was for real."

For a year, King and her husband spoke frequently with Gibson on the phone. They went to visit him in Pennsylvania in 2003. Together they went to the Vietnam Wall, where they placed a book commemorating Clark's life.

Gibson told them how Clark volunteered to lead his squad as it worked its way toward higher ground that fateful day in Vietnam.

Fate as in the loss of Clark and as in what spared Gibson, who had asked to serve as a medic after being drafted. Instead, the Army sent him to learn electronics, specifically radios.

"Jim was up front," Gibson said. "He was hit."

Shot in the chest, Clark died instantly. Brian Cannada, the medic who was there because the Army had other plans for Gibson, didn't know Clark was dead when he responded to his first casualty in the field. He rushed up to help the fallen sergeant. He, too, was shot and killed.

Because of his electronics training, Gibson was handed a radio when another radioman was shot. He had to stay toward the back of the unit to keep in touch with the command post. He knew from the chatter up ahead someone had been shot and immediately feared it was Clark.

"That was the last time we attempted to probe up a mountain instead of down," Gibson said. "I slept that night next to their bodies. It was too late to take them out."

And too late for Clark's mother and father, who both died before Gibson contacted the family.

"My parents needed (to hear) it, but they didn't survive," King said.

Gibson has visited the Kings and other family members twice, coming to Modesto in 2007 and again in September 2009. He has tried to find the family of the slain medic, Cannada, with no luck.

That Gibson located the Kings became even more important just a few weeks ago, when Marti King was diagnosed with lymphoma and leukemia. She is in a local hospital.

"It was a just a miracle," Marti said. "He found us. He's given us a whole new idea of life and how it was (in Vietnam). It means a lot to me to know that Jim had a buddy -- a nice buddy, and he is a buddy."

Gibson said the miracle is being able to give part of Jim Clark back to his family, if only through an understanding of the way he died. He only wishes Jim's mom and dad could have been there to hear it, too.

Now, 42 years later, the death of Sgt. James Clark still resonates within these families: The Clarks and Kings, who now know what happened, and the Gibsons, because Brian Gibson is no longer a dead man walking.

"I can cry about it now," he said. "I know what stirs my heart, my emotions. I know what it is and I can tell somebody about it. I'm so thankful I can talk about it."

Anonymous for 43 years, rescuer meets the pilot he saved

March 6, 2011

Wayne Hague always wondered whatever happened to the pilot whose crippled plane he refueled and escorted to safety over North Vietnam in 1967.

Ron Catton always wondered about that pilot who kept him from having to bail out of his F-4C Phantom fighter and into a suite at the "Hanoi Hilton," the nickname for an infamous North Vietnamese prison.

More than 43 years passed since their meeting in the sky over Southeast Asia linked them, even though they never knew each other's name. But fate has a way of working things out.

This head-spinner happened because two men who live more than 900 miles apart told their versions of same story to the same people who helped them connect.

Bart Ah You / The Modesto Bee
KC-135 pilot Wayne Hague.

Here's the gist of it:

Hague is a counselor at the Merced County Rescue Mission in Merced.

Catton, 78, owns a financial services business in Spokane, Wash.

In December, Catton spoke to a group of students at Riverside Christian High School, which his grandchildren attend in Yakima, Wash. He regaled them with stories of flying with the Thunderbirds, the Air Force's precision aerial team. He also told them about his near catastrophe during the war and how a pilot and crew of a KC-135 refueling plane disobeyed orders by flying about 100 miles into North Vietnam to get him.

That story sounded familiar to Rick Van Beek, the school's principal. Van Beek had heard it from his wife, Lolly, who heard it from the tanker pilot during a medical missionary trip to Kenya. He heard it again from Paul Emmons, the Yakima doctor who helped organize the Kenya trip, during a dinner at the Van Beeks' home.

"The bells started going off in my head," Van Beek said. "How can these be separate stories?"

Seeing Catton again at a basketball game a couple of weeks later, Van Beek went to his office and called his daughter, who also went on the Africa trip. She knew the tanker pilot's name. Van Beek then did a Google

Courtesy of Ron Catton

Vietnam War F-4 pilot Ron Catton.

search on Wayne Hague. He printed the information, returned to the gym and handed it to Catton.

"I said, 'Here's another pilot who seems to have the other half of your story,' " Van Beek told him.

Not so fast. Let's back up a bit to the fall of 1967.

Catton served in the 8th Tactical Fighter Wing under the highly decorated Col. Robin Olds. Military buffs will know that Olds claimed 12 dogfight kills in World War II and four more over Vietnam. A football star at West Point, he later married actress Ella Raines and retired as a brigadier general in the Air Force. On this particular day, Catton flew the lead plane among Phantoms providing cover for bombers on a mission over Hanoi.

Once the bombers emptied their loads, they returned to their bases. Then the Phantoms zoomed down and dropped their bombs as well.

As Catton bombed a railroad bridge, enemy rounds ripped into the intake of his right engine.

"All of that debris went through the engine and wiped it out," Catton said. "My fire warning light was on. I jinked to the left, jinked to my right. I looked over my shoulder and there were three MiGs on me."

One MiG had drawn other U.S. fighters and acted as a decoy, leaving those three to pounce on Catton's crippled plane.

Catton took his fighter into a hard vertical climb, then came back down and flew right through their formation.

Olds, who had been chasing the first MiG, gave up a chance for a kill to run off the three that were after Catton's plane.

"Here he came, lobbing missiles over my head at the MiGs," Catton said.

The MiGs high-tailed it, with Olds in pursuit.

That threat subsided, Catton still faced another: a plane with one blown-out engine and other major problems, including the fact that he was still above North Vietnamese real estate.

"I was heading back toward Laos, all shot up and leaking fuel," Catton said. "I wanted to bail out over Laos. If I bailed (over North Vietnam), I would have ended up in the Hanoi Hilton."

He put out what amounted to a mayday call, and Hague, flying over Laos in his KC-135, answered.

"When I heard his voice," Catton said, "it was like the voice of God. I told him I was heading west toward Laos. He said, 'Negative, Cadillac Lead (Catton's code name). I'll come and get you.' "

Just one problem: Hague had strict orders not to cross over the border into North Vietnam.

With a pilot in trouble, though, he didn't hesitate. But Hague didn't simply stick the nose of his plane over the border. He hooked up with Catton over the Black River, roughly 100 miles from Laos.

"I just went in and got him," Hague said.

As they positioned their respective planes to connect the refueling boom, Catton radioed: "Understand, I've got a fire warning and smoke in the cockpit. You don't have to take me on."

Hague's response?

"Cadillac lead, get your sorry ass in position for a hook-up before I change my mind!"

Catton's plane leaked the fuel as quickly as the tanker could pump it in. So they stayed connected for more than 200 miles until Catton detached to land at the Udon air base in Thailand. Just as Catton touched down, his left engine quit, too. Hague returned to his air base at Takhli.

Hague never told anyone at Takhli about the incident. Someone else must have. His superiors knew, and the rumor mill soon began to churn.

A day or so later, on the ground at Udon, Catton heard that the tanker pilot likely would be court-martialed for going over into North Vietnam, putting his crew and plane at severe risk. So Catton went to Olds, who had a simple solution to the problem: He'd recommend the tanker pilot for a Silver Star.

Neither Hague nor Catton can say this for certain, but both heard the Silver Star recommendation arrived at headquarters the same day as the court-martial papers, leaving the brass to weigh an act of heroism that saved a pilot's life against the military crime of blatantly disobeying orders.

Hague never got his Silver Star, but he didn't get court-martialed, either.

"It washed," Hague said.

Through all of this, neither Hague nor Catton learned each other's identity. Catton, in fact, later wrote about the incident, referring to Hague as "Big Boy 31," a name he made up for Hague in lieu of knowing his real one. It stayed that way until Feb. 6, when Hague got a phone call that went something like this:

"Are you Wayne Hague?"

"Yes, I am," he answered.

"Were you in Vietnam in 1967?" the caller continued.

"Yes, I was."

"Did you enter North Vietnam to pick up a fighter pilot, shot up and going down?"

"Yes, I did."

"I'm the pilot."

Only then did Hague learn the name of the man he had rescued more than 43 years ago.

They met a few days later. Hague already planned on traveling to Lewiston, Idaho, to watch grandson Jason Hague play baseball at Lewis-Clark State College. So he drove two more hours to Spokane, and they saw each other face to face for the first time -- safe, sound and on the ground.

Hague always wondered about the fighter pilot whose life he saved so long ago.

Likewise with Catton.

"All this time, it's been, 'Gee, I wish I knew who it was,' " Catton said. "Then to have it happen like that. He's a really nice guy."

And a lifesaver.

Hague lives in Merced. Catton lives in Spokane, WA.

Ron Grantski wants the world to know what happened to the USS Liberty in a 1967 attack.

50 years later, truth still matters to USS Liberty crewman who survived attack by Israelis

May 27, 2017

In 1982, after the first reunion of the USS Liberty Veterans Association Ron Grantski returned to his Modesto home and flipped on the phone's message recorder.

Several played, and then this one: "You'd better stop talking about the USS Liberty and Israel," Grantski recalls the voice saying. "Something will happen to you."

Nothing's happened. Grantski is still here at 70 years old. He believes the best way he can honor 34 shipmates killed when unmarked Israeli fighter planes and torpedo boats attacked the super-secret spy ship on June 8, 1967, in the Mediterranean Sea is to speak his mind about the attack and the coverup that followed. Memorial Day, he said, is as good as any to do so after being told for decades to shut up.

Grantski and others believe the attack was intentional, that Israel did not as it claimed mistake the USS Liberty for another ship when it tried to sink it on the fourth day of the Six Days War.

Israel later admitted to the attack. It paid more than $3.2 million to the families of those killed and over $3.5 million to 74 of the wounded by 1969. Then, in 1980, it paid the U.S. $6 million for damages to the ship's communications equipment. But the governments of Israel and the U.S. refuse to say the attack was purposeful even though cryptographers and techs aboard the Liberty – including Grantski – intercepted messages they believe inferred the Israelis staged the attack to make it look like Egypt or other members of the Arab coalition did it in order to draw the U.S. into the war on Israel's side.

"I had top-secret crypto clearance – the highest you could get," Grantski said. His job was to copy the messages transmitted. "They would change the station in the middle of a message and someone else would say, 'Ski, he's on .. ' whatever station, and I'd switch to that one.' They were using lots of Morse Code, and sending at 50 to 70 words per minute, which is pretty darned fast to be copying in code."

One message in particular stood out.

"I had intercepted a message the Israelis were going to attack (a U.S.) base and blame it on the Arabs, or implied so," he said. The message forwarded as top-secret to the White House. "Unbeknownst to us, it was our ship that was going to be attacked."

He'd just finished his shift and was smoking a cigarette on the fantail when the captain sounded the call to general quarters. In came the fighter planes with their 20 mm cannons blasting away, some dropping napalm that sent the crew scrambling to get below deck.

Grantski felt the burning of the napalm on his hands and later took shrapnel in the buttocks, wounds for which he received a Purple Heart.

The gunners front and midship had no chance, he said, holding an armor-piercing bullet he'd found on the deck after the attack. "This one was a dud."

Then the torpedo boats came upon them.

"The captain had the ship zig-zagging," he said. "They fired five torpedoes. One hit."

It blew a huge hole in the side. The crew closed the hatches to keep the ship afloat, but most of those killed were below deck.

"I was down there on my first cruise," Grantski said. "If I had still be down there, I'd have been dead. The captain (William L. McGonagle) was wounded. He ran the ship on his back, with an aide holding a megaphone so he could give orders."

At one point, someone told the crew to prepare to abandon ship – an order McGonagle quickly overruled.

"He said, 'Gentlemen,' " Grantski recalled, " 'get to your battle stations. We are not abandoning ship.' "

The attack, according to accounts, lasted about 80 minutes though it seemed much longer to those aboard. U.S. fighter planes never arrived to drive off the attackers. Grantski said the image of the fires, the blood and carnage are etched in his mind forever.

"It was 50 years ago, and its sharp like it was yesterday," he said.

So is the memory of the message left on his answering machine when he returned from the reunion in 1982. Hearing it chilled him, he admits, because he knew there was a chance whoever uttered it wasn't kidding. Other crew members received similar calls, he said.

He muted his educated opinions to protect the family he and partner Sharon Rocha raised in Modesto. (Rocha's daughter, Laci Peterson, was murdered in 2002 by husband Scott Peterson in a case than drew national attention.)

But those days are over for Grantski and those who believe the Israeli attack not only was intentional, but also that the Johnson administration likely ordered the coverup, ruled accidental in a game of international politics. Grantski isn't alone. Admiral Thomas H. Moorer wrote a detailed 1997 memorandum that is posted on USSLiberty.org.

A couple of passages from that document:

"Israel knew perfectly well that the ship was American. After all, the *Liberty*'s American flag and markings were in full view in perfect visibility for the Israeli aircraft that overflew the ship eight times over a period of nearly eight hours prior to the attack," Moorer wrote. "I am confident that Israel knew the Liberty could intercept radio messages from all parties and potential parties to the ongoing war, then in its fourth day, and that Israel was preparing to seize the Golan Heights from Syria despite President Johnson's known opposition to such a move. I think they realized that if we learned in advance of their plan, there would be a tremendous amount of negotiating between Tel Aviv and Washington."

And Moorer questioned why U.S. air support for the ship never arrived.

"In the *Liberty* case, fighters were put in the air not once, but twice. They were ordered to stand down by Secretary of Defense McNamara and President Johnson for reasons the American public deserves to know," Thomas wrote. "The captain and crew of the *Liberty*, rather than being widely acclaimed as the heroes they most certainly are, have been silenced, ignored, honored belatedly and away from the cameras, and denied a history that accurately reflects their ordeal."

The USS Liberty Association will meet in Norfolk, Va., on Wednesday to mark the 50-year anniversary of the attack. Only 20 then, the 70-year-old Grantski has health problems that will prevent him from joining the 150 or so surviving crew members. He will be with them in spirit, though, and half a century later his goal remains unchanged.

"It's important that the true story comes out," he said.

Grantski lives in Modesto.

Medic's severe war injury creates whole new battle

December 25, 2005

She's constantly trying to jog his memory, trying to fill in gaps caused by the bomb that nearly killed him.

So one day, when Athena Ferguson mentioned to her husband that they had been married for 16 years, his reply caught her by surprise. Utter shock, actually.

"He looked at me seriously and said, 'I'm not married,' " she said. "I was frustrated. I said, 'Who do you think has been doing all of this?' "

And then she saw a smile crease her husband's face. And at that moment, she knew that while Sgt. James Ferguson no longer could move the left side of his body, the bomb didn't get his sense of humor.

He'd duped her.

"Got her good," James Ferguson said with a smile, sitting in his wheelchair in their Tracy home and continuing to tease her. "That was my escape right there."

"He was like his old self again, " Athena Ferguson said.

The Fergusons needed the laugh and certainly deserved it. In April, the Army National Guard medic volunteered to pull gunner's duty in Baghdad. While on patrol, Ferguson's Humvee hit a bomb that sent shrapnel into the right side of his head. He survived only because some members of his unit drove the burning Humvee back to the base hospital. Soon after, he was flown to Germany.

Since then, Athena Ferguson has fought a two-front war, battling Army officials to get the proper benefits, care and equipment for her husband, while leaving behind the life they knew.

She has been relentless in her attempts to navigate the Army's no-man's land of bureaucracy and slow-motion protocol. She can't understand why it's taking so long to get her husband the custom electric wheelchair and accessories he needs, along with the proper lifting device to move him out of the chair and into bed.

"He's 6-foot-3 (215 pounds) and I'm 5 feet," she said. "What happens if I hurt my back lifting him? What do we do then?"

She spent $3,900 to buy him a bed and $2,500 for a special shower wheelchair.

She brought him home from the Veterans Affairs medical campus in Livermore because they had him in a nursing facility that provided limited options for physical and occupational therapy.

"He didn't need to be in a nursing home," she said. "The people there (Livermore) were doing their best. It was just not the place he should have been."

Does a soldier -- a reservist sent into battle and injured for life while fighting for his country -- deserve this kind of treatment? Shouldn't they get more in the way of answers than, "you need to be more patient," Athena Ferguson wondered.

"I'm on a need-to-know basis," she said.

But she fears that if she complains too loudly, the Army will slow down an already tedious and frustrating process even more.
"It's a Catch-22," she said.

Now, Athena Ferguson takes her husband to Sutter Tracy Community Hospital most days to get the therapy he's needed since arriving home Thanksgiving Day from a hospital in Bethesda, Md.

"He's made some big strides since he's been home," she said.

The adjustment has been and will continue to be difficult. She moved the family to Tracy to be closer to the Livermore facility before realizing that wasn't the best option. She still home-schools their 14-year-old daughter, Jacinda. Their Oakdale home is up for sale while they're living in a rented home equipped for wheelchair access.

The injury affected James Ferguson's short-term memory, so his wife works constantly to close the gap between the past and the present.

"We're making progress," she said.

James Ferguson can look at photos taken in Iraq and describe in great detail the people and places in them.

He can recall Christmases past and the gatherings with family. He can remember going four-wheeling with friends and many other things from more than a year ago.

"He has long-term memory," Athena Ferguson said. "That, I'm really grateful for. If he didn't have that, I don't know."

What he can't remember, an hour or so later, is that he just looked at those pictures. Nor can he remember anything that happened since the time his unit -- the 184th Infantry Regiment -- was called up in August 2004.

"I can't remember being over there (Iraq)," he said. "After several months, you'd think I'd remember something."

It takes something visual -- the photos - to trigger his memory.

He does remember many things, including working for a bottled-water company and preparing to enter Modesto Junior College's nursing program. He's looking forward to the day when he can go four-wheeling with friends again.

"I'll never give that up," he said.

The Christmas tree in the corner of their home is adorned with lights, ornaments and presents. His gift, however, is his attitude and resilience that will serve him well on the long road ahead.

"I'm glad for the fact that I'm home," he said. "I think about the guys who are over there, and it bums me out. But I don't regret being in the military even though I am like I am now. I refuse to live my life with regrets."

And if he can lighten things up by teasing his wife, she's perfectly OK with that.

The Fergusons live in Sonora.

Riverbank parents learn mistakes by military cost son's life

February 21, 2010

The 500-page report, two inches thick, rests on the table in Nikki Freitas' Riverbank home.

She can't bring herself to read it word for word, to anguish over every last detail of how her son, 22-year-old Navy Petty Officer James Layton, died in an ambush last September in Afghanistan's Ganjgal Valley.

Maybe someday perhaps, but not now. Too much painful information. The words in it cannot bring her son back to life, back home to Riverbank and back into a loving mother's embrace.

A general came to her home three weeks ago to confirm what she and Brent Layton -- her ex-husband and James' father -- already knew: Their son, three Marines and an Army sergeant ultimately died because the upper command made a series of deadly decisions as exposed by McClatchy reporter Jonathan Landay, who was on the ground with James Layton and his unit when the ambush occurred.

And while Layton's family members were initially told by some military officials to disregard Landay's published accounts, Marine Brig. Gen. James Laster set the record straight.

"The general told us personally that Jonathan's reporting was right on the money," Brent Layton said. "They flat came out and said, 'We screwed up.' "

The report -- which Brent Layton is in the process of reading thoroughly -- detailed virtually everything that happened in the Sept. 8 ambush. It tells how James Layton was shot by insurgents who wore flak jackets, Afghanistan army gear and carried recoil-less rifles -- as he tended to a wounded soldier.

"They were well-equipped and well-placed," Brent Layton said.

James was shot in the right eye from a distance of about 30 feet, and died instantly.

"It's very emotional to read it," Brent Layton said. "It puts it in terms of minute by minute, step by step."

"Second by second," added Gilbert Freitas, Nikki's husband and James' stepfather.

"Stuff you don't want to know and at the same time, things you need to know," Brent Layton said.

"It's like a bad movie, and we're in the middle of it. It really rehashes that day."

The report also explains how leaders of the operation failed to provide artillery and air support. It reveals pure chaos in the communications between the commanders in the operations center and those in the field, blaming two unnamed majors for many of the breakdowns.

Men 'died bravely'

The bottom line, Brent Layton said, is that the military's upper command completely botched the operation.

"Pencil pushers calling a war from behind a desk," he said. "We grieve as parents, knowing things could have been prevented. It's sickening. It's a circus. It shouldn't be that way."

But that doesn't detract from anything James Layton or the others did on the ground, he said.

"These men died bravely," Brent Layton said. "We need to remember these men are heroes. That's what it needs to be about. They did what they were supposed to do. The guys upstairs did not. I have 100 percent confidence in the Marines, Army and Navy people on the ground. I will never have confidence in the military's upper commands again."

Even so, Layton's family members say they are fortunate to have an accurate accounting of how he died.

They credit Landay's reporting for forcing the military to tell the truth -- unlike the lies and misinformation former NFL player Pat Tillman's family endured when the Army tried to cover up the fact he had been killed by friendly fire.

Not this time, Gilbert Freitas said.

"Because that reporter was out there," he said, "they could not embellish it or say anything false."

The family hopes the deaths of James and the others will force the military brass to put measures in place to prevent others on the ground from being sacrificed by ineptitude. Just as she cannot bear to read the 500-page report, Nikki Freitas no longer reads newspaper accounts or watches reports of the war on TV. She prefers to remember the loving son who joined the Navy to become a medic, to aid wounded Marines on the ground, and who wanted to go to Afghanistan.

"He said Afghanistan was beautiful -- that if you could find the garden of Eden, that's where it would have been," she said. "The mountains, the different landscapes. He was so amazed by it."

His death left a hole in her heart no report can fill.

"He's my son," Nikki Freitas said. "That's how I look at him."

Brent Layton, James Layton's father, died in 2015.

Family's War Worries Go On Leave as Son Comes Home for Christmas

12/16/2003

While her son tended to wounded soldiers in Iraq, Malinda Martinez fought her own private war at home in Modesto.

She worried about the safety of Michael Martinez, a Navy corpsman who was on the ground when the Marines stormed the Baghdad airport in April. Malinda, husband Carlos and the rest of their family worried mostly because of what they didn't know -- the fierceness of the battle, the danger. And had they known more, they would have worried even more.

Michael Martinez, 22, was in the thick of the fighting, carrying not a rifle but a medic's bag.

The unknown -- that is the most difficult thing about being the proud parents of a person serving in the military, the Martinezes said.
They know the most important thing now: He's safe, he's sound and he's home.

Michael stepped off a United twin-prop plane Monday afternoon and ambled through the door of the Modesto Airport. The 1999 Johansen High graduate received a hero's welcome resplendent with hugs and kisses, tears and laughter, hand-made signs and cheers. More than 30 friends and relatives gathered to greet him.

Their reunion moved other folks who had come to the airport to pick up their own family members, friends or business associates. Airport manager Van Switzer, who had never met the Martinezes, stepped forward to thank Michael for serving his country.

It all caught Michael by surprise.

"I had no idea. I thought it was just going to be the five of them," he said, referring to his parents, his brother Daniel, a freshman at Johansen High; and his sister Christina, a law student at Humphreys College, and her boyfriend.

Michael is home for the holidays, on leave from Camp Lejeune, N.C. until Jan. 10. It's his first time back in Modesto in 13 months, and the first time he's seen his family since February. He'll have the opportunity to tell them what he couldn't say for security reasons while he was in Iraq and Algeria.

"It was hard, not knowing what was going on," his father, Carlos said. "He couldn't tell us where he was or what he was doing."

There were occasional e-mails that contained hints. His parents literally had to break code to get beyond the words and into the meaning of his messages.

"He'd say everything was brown," Malinda said. "He said the flies were taking off and landing. That was his way of telling us he was on the ground (at the airport in Iraq). Or he'd talk about the blue -- the whales, the ocean. That's when we knew he was aboard ship (the carrier USS Iwo Jima)."

The e-mails stopped when the fighting began, and no news became the best news.

"When I heard the Marines landed, I went home from work," said Malinda, a receptionist at Sutter Gould Medical Center in Modesto. "I stayed home for the next two days. I couldn't handle it."

She and Jane Hutton of Modesto, whose son serves on a submarine, leaned on each other for support. Their sons -- both named Michael -- are best friends and attended Johansen High School together.

The Martinezes didn't hear from their Michael for roughly three months. During that time, he worried, too, but about the Marines doing the fighting. He can now tell them what it was like to be at the airport, waiting for pleas for help.

"I'm there listening for 'Corpsman up!' or 'Doc!' or somebody screaming," said Michael, who plans to become a doctor someday. "You wonder if you're able to respond quickly enough."

When the fighting slowed, his thoughts -- his worries -- turned to home.

"I knew my dad has problems with his back," he said. "I wondered how he was doing. I wondered how my sister was doing at school and work. I wondered how my brother was doing, that football season was starting. I tried to keep my mind occupied."

They can now tell him they, too, are OK – that fretting for the safety of the young man they love so much was the toughest part.

And when they found out he would be coming home for the holidays, the worry became anticipation, which is a polite way of saying impatience.

"I haven't slept," Malinda Martinez said in the minutes before his plane landed. "I haven't eaten. I'm taking Thursday and Friday off to be with him."

Her own private war is over. For the next 25 days, at least, she can quit worrying. Her son is home for Christmas.

Acknowledgments

This book would not have been possible without the willingness of the people who shared their experiences, opened their hearts and memory vaults. They told their stories in ways that brought home the camaraderie, the horrors of battle, their sacrifices, the moods of the times and the emotional remnants they carried with them -- many for decades until their deaths.

Nor would it have been possible without the support of The Modesto Bee, which entrusted me with what I considered the best job at the newspaper, and in a profession more vital than ever to the American way of life. Thanks go to now-retired Editor Mark Vasche, late Managing Editor Joe Demma (who elevated me into the columnist role), current Editor Joe Kieta, Publisher Ken Riddick, retired Opinions Page Editor Judy Sly, and Mike Dunbar, current Opinions Page Editor and friend of four decades. They all supported the need to tell these stories while the veterans are or were still around to do so.

Photographers Joan Barnett Lee, Debbie Noda, Bart Ah You, Ted Benson, Al Golub, Steve Kosko and Brian Ramsay took the photos that helped tell these stories.

Artist and former co-worker Laurie McAdam designed the book's covers.

Godson William Dunbar served as my IT director, cleaning up the messes I made on the computer.

And finally, thanks go to Publisher Riddick and Editor Kieta for granting me permission to use the columns and photos, which remain the intellectual property of The Modesto Bee.

About the Author

Jeff Jardine recently retired from a 39-year career in journalism, the last 29 years at the Modesto Bee and 14 of those as the local columnist.

As a sports columnist, he covered three Super Bowls, three World Series, NBA playoffs and scores of world championship fights. He moved from sports to news in 1996 and covered everything from natural disasters to major crime cases including the Yosemite tourists murders, the Chandra Levy and Scott Peterson cases.

He earned numerous awards including best columnist by both the California Newspaper Publishers Association and the Associated Press News Editors, and appeared on "Dateline NBC" and "ABC 20-20."

A native of Sonora, CA, he lives in Oakdale with his wife, Sandra, and daughter Erin.